THE ULTIMATE TRUE CRIME PUZZLE BOOK

Over 100 Killer Activities for True Crime and Serial Killer Fanatics

JACK ROSEWOOD

D1534591

ISBN: 978-1-64845-098-3
Copyright © 2023 by LAK Publishing
ALL RIGHTS RESERVED

No part of this book may be reproduced, stored in a retrieval system, or transmitted in any form or by any means, electronic, mechanical, photocopying, recording, scanning, or otherwise, without the prior written permission of the publisher.

Free Bonus Books

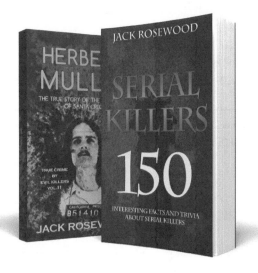

Get two free True Crime books when you
join Jack Rosewood's newsletter over at
www.JackRosewood.com/free

CONTENTS

CONTENTS

CONTENTS

INTRODUCTION

True Crime has exploded in popularity in the last decade. It seems like you can't do anything without being met with a never-ending list of podcasts, documentaries, books, movies, and TV series dedicated to both short overviews and scarily detailed deep dives into every true crime topic known to man. It can be overwhelming, but if you're anything like me, you try and consume as much of it as possible!

What makes these stories so interesting? As upsetting as these cases can be, why do we continue reading, listening, and watching from the edge of our seats?

Some would say it's simply morbid curiosity. We gawk at the grotesque and wonder how another human being could think and act so wildly different from the rest of us. Others consider it a form of protection; maybe knowing how the enemy thinks and moves could guard us against them.

For many, though, a true crime fascination is about the thrill of the chase. We play detective right alongside the real heroes of these stories: the people who tirelessly investigate humanity's darkest impulses in the hopes of finding a happy ending for victims and their families. It is thrilling to follow along, use our own detective skills, keep our minds sharp, and collect the clues. We love using our existing knowledge and getting to build on it.

It's ultimately about finding a solution. We are compelled to stick it out, because hearing about the resolution to even the most horrific of stories is supremely satisfying.

When you get right down to it, solving puzzles like the ones contained in this book is a lot like solving a real-life crime. You have to keep your eyes open for clues, draw on your previous knowledge of a subject, and put all the pieces together to find a solution. Plus, in the end, the excitement of solving a mystery, whether big or small, will always leave you feeling electrified.

Perhaps that's why one of the world's most famous and beloved detectives, Sherlock Holmes, said, "My mind rebels at stagnation, give me problems, give me work!" OK, so he may not be a real detective, but he's still got a point. Not using your brain is boring! And it certainly won't make you a better crime-solver. So enjoy using your detective skills, and all the true crime knowledge you've collected, to solve these puzzles!

HEAVY HITTERS

NOTORIOUS KILLERS #1

DOWN

1. Ted Bundy provided authorities with psychological insight into the case of this other killer

2. Woman who allegedly murdered her father and stepmother with an axe

3. Unknown killer who promised not to murder any residents of New Orleans if they had a jazz band playing

4. Murderer with an astrological nickname

5. Oklahoma man who killed his cellmate because he wanted to be sentenced to death

6. Killer notorious for targeting women with brown hair, parted down the middle

7. Elizabeth Short is also known by this floral nickname

9. Killer who only murdered people with unlocked doors, believing that locked doors were a sign that he wasn't welcome there

12. Woodland creature that could possibly have led to the death of Kathleen Peterson

13. Killer who opened Chicago's "murder castle"

ACROSS

8. Known as "The Confession Killer," man who falsely admitted to killing as many as 600 people

10. Austrian killer who wrote about the murders he was committing

11. Killer whose last meal on death row included food from a restaurant he used to manage

14. Serial killer who inserted metal rods into his abdomen and groin

15. One of The Golden State Killer's original monikers

NOTORIOUS KILLERS #2

DOWN

1. 450-pound killer who owned a food stand where he may have served human flesh
2. Name for the romantic attraction to criminals
3. The term "bystander effect" is often used in regard to this woman's murder
4. New career Ed Kemper began in prison
6. Woman who shot and killed her own children, and blamed it on a carjacker
7. Historically, the country with the most serial killers

ACROSS

5. Jeffrey Dahmer's morbid childhood hobby
8. Country where Canadian killer Luka Magnotta was apprehended
9. Dahmer avoided victims with this kind of body modification, claiming it made the flesh taste weird
10. What needs to happen between murders for them to be classified as a serial killings
11. Car Donald "Pee-Wee" Gaskins drove
12. One of the most common methods of killing used by serial killers
13. Doctor who is potentially England's most prolific serial killer, with a possible 200+ victims

KILLING GROUNDS

Identify the killing grounds of 20 killers.

1. Ted Bundy's last murders (Tallahassee, Florida, U.S.A.)

2. Robert Pickton (British Columbia, Canada)

3. Dennis Nilsen (London, England)

4. Jeffrey Dahmer (Milwaukee, Wisconsin, U.S.A.)

5. Andrei Chikatilo (Rostov Oblast, Russia)

6. Juana Barraza (Mexico City, Mexico)

7. Peter Kürten (Düsseldorf, Germany)

8. David and Catherine Birnie (Perth, Australia)

9. Jack Unterweger (Austria)

10. Yang Xinhai (Henan, China)

11. Pedro Alonso López (Colombia)

12. Yvan Keller (France)

13. Zsuzsanna Fazekas and the Angel Makers (Hungary)

14. Mohan Kumar (India)

15. Beasts of Satan (Lombardy, Italy)

16. Nikolai Dzhumagaliev (Kazakhstan)

17. Frans Hooijmaijers (Limburg, Netherlands)

18. Javed Iqbal (Pakistan)

19. Paweł Alojzy Tuchlin (Poland)

20. Lê Thanh Vân (Vietnam)

KILLERS' JOBS

Crime doesn't pay! Literally. Even killers need a day job. Can you unscramble these words to reveal some of the surprisingly wholesome jobs famous killers have had? Look to the hints at the bottom to see who had what job.

1. **EIC RMCAE TUKRC DIRREV** _____
2. **CLEPIO EIRCOFF** _____
3. **SYRIUTEC SMSYTE ITLASRLNE** _____
4. **HTBLNGUIC WNOSRE** _____
5. **HTO DGO NOVRDE** _____
6. **HREFTEGRIIF** _____
7. **BYRHITAD OLCWN** _____
8. **NJLOUARTIS** _____
9. **YGPAOHRRNOP CRATO** _____
10. **ASUNSRI GEGAANLU CRTEEHA** _____
11. **KCF NHRIAECSF AAGERMN** _____
12. **RVADEGEGIRG** _____
13. **DCEIISU EOIPVENTNR LNETIHO** _____
14. **ERALSDNAPC** _____
15. **AMLL ATSNA** _____
16. **SMCUI MORPOETR** _____
17. **IGP EFRAMR** _____
18. **SIFSLREPOONA RLTERSEW** _____
19. **IBSBYARTTE** _____
20. **TOCOELHAC YFTORCA ERRKWO** _____

▶▶▶ DO NOT CROSS ◀◀◀   ▶▶▶ STOP ◀◀◀   ▶▶▶ DO NOT CROSS ◀◀◀   ▶▶▶ STOP ◀◀◀   ▶▶▶ DO NOT CROSS ◀◀◀

HINTS!

1. Fred West
2. Joseph DeAngelo
3. Dennis Rader
4. The Krays
5. Carl Grossmann
6. Nikolai Dzhumagaliev

7. John Wayne Gacy
8. Jack Unterweger
9. Luka Magnotta
10. Andrei Chikatilo
11. John Wayne Gacy (again!)
12. Peter Sutcliffe
13. Ted Bundy

14. Bruce McArthur
15. Bruce McArthur (again!)
16. Wayne Williams
17. Robert Pickton
18. Juana Barraza
19. Ed Gein
20. Jeffrey Dahmer

KILLERS' NAMES

```
X H V R N O L I T A K I H C I E R D N A H S Q J
S U G D E K M R U H T R A C M E C U R B R N Y D
Y X C E W G R W J P H J J B I S F W A O J Z N M
L N J N S U E F W C B Y E N C P U T M O Z I N V
Y N J N W Q M W C V H P N E Y I W S S N K P O K
E Q Y I M A H K R Q T A F R L T S E G O R N T H
Z B O S C Y A B G E M G P A C N P T L W E A K A
E V I R J F D P P S T B M T D H O A U B T R C Z
F Z F A E U Y C S D K N G F D I I B J T Z P I A
F C K D L B E O C K N S U E J D O O O H Y R P R
I W D E G D R B I V Z Y A K Z L H N L G V T T R
L A A R K G F Z M O L N U H C N G J H A D B R A
C U E Y L N F K W M G V U H W A O U B J X U E B
T R T R N K E E E E G M U A M Y J R S Z B N B A
U S A E U E J H L X A M Y A H C J M Y V I V O N
S C K H D Y W O T G U N K H J Y L O J H F A R A
R O Q O A B Y I A O E U T J K R A Y T W I N S U
E H V K Z N U L L G L V V B T V F J Y F M G S J
T T M H C J I N A L F C X X Q X G U X B M P Q A
E E B P K E M C D I I J L L O P Z T F C J V S X
P A H O V C Y V V Y Y A A N I E G D E V H N T U B
I E J E T S E W D E R F M S V P C P Q W Q E L H
A N F T L A D R V O E X I S R S F J N Z D F I S
I J T D L A A P N Z G D Q G G H K X E E P U P Q
```

LUKA MAGNOTTA   **NIKOLAI DZHUMAGALIEV**   **CARL GROSSMANN**   **WAYNE WILLIAMS**

PETER SUTCLIFFE   **JUANA BARRAZA**   **ANDREI CHIKATILO**   **BRUCE MCARTHUR**   **KRAY TWINS**

JEFFREY DAHMER   **ROBERT PICKTON**   **ED GEIN**   **JOHN WAYNE GACY**   **DENNIS RADER**

JOSEPH DEANGELO   **JACK UNTERWEGER**   **TED BUNDY**   **FRED WEST**

KILLERS' LAST WORDS #1

A cryptogram is a puzzle where one letter of the alphabet is replaced with another. For example, in this first puzzle, all Es have been replaced with Ys, all Hs are Js, and all Ps are Ls. Use your detective skills to deduce what all the other letters stand for, solve the puzzles below, and reveal some of the sinister, confusing, and morbidly funny things killers have said as their last words!

A	B	C	D	E	F	G	H	I	J	K	L	M	N	O	P	Q	R	S	T	U	V	W	X	Y	Z
				Y			J								L										

```
_ E _ _     _ E     _ _ _ E _     _ _     H E _ _     H _ _     _ E E _
Z Y U U     T Y     P R Z Y E     T C     J Y P M     J P X     K Y Y O

_ H _ P P E _     _ _ _     _ _ _ _     _     _ _ _ _ _     _ E
Q J G L L Y M     G R R     B V U U     V     X Z V U U     K Y

_ _ _ E     _ _     H E _ _     _ _     _ E _ _ _     _ _ _     _
P K U Y     Z G     J Y P E     P Z     U Y P X Z     R G E     P

_ _ _ E _ _     _ H E     _ _ _ _ _     _ _     _ _     _ _ _
T G T Y O Z     Z J Y     X G D O M     G R     T C     G B O

_ _ _ _ _     _ _ _ H _ _ _     _ _ _ _     _ H E     _ _ _ _ P
K U G G M     S D X J V O S     R E G T     Z J Y     X Z D T L

_ _     _ _     _ E _ ?     _ H _ _     _ _ _ _ _     _ E _
G R     T C     O Y Q A     Z J P Z     B G D U M     K Y     P

P _ E _ _ _ _ E     _ _     E _ _     _ _ _     P _ E _ _ _ _ E _
L U Y P X D E Y     Z G     Y O M     P U U     L U Y P X D E Y X
```

- Peter Kürten -

KILLERS' LAST WORDS #2

>>> DO NOT CROSS <<< >>> STOP <<< >>> DO NOT CROSS <<< >>> STOP <<< >>> DO NOT CROSS <<<

>>> DO NOT CROSS <<< >>> STOP <<< >>> DO NOT CROSS <<< >>> STOP <<< >>> DO NOT CROSS <<<

A	B	C	D	E	F	G	H	I	J	K	L	M	N	O	P	Q	R	S	T	U	V	W	X	Y	Z
								E	W																

I'_ J___ _I __ ___ I'_ _I__I_
E P W T L C Q E J Z C Y L B D E N L B E Q E R K

_I ___ ____ ___ I'_ _I ____
V E C O C O Z U Y F J B R P E Q Q I Z I B F J

_I__ _I_____ ___ _I__
Q E J Z E R P Z S R P Z R F Z P B D V E C O

J____ J___ 6. _I__ ___ ___I_,
W Z L T L W T R Z   Q E J Z C O Z N Y H E Z

_I_ _____ ___I ___ ___, I'__
I E K N Y C O Z U L O E S B R P B Q Q E Q Q

__ ____.
I Z I B F J

- Aileen Wuornos -

KILLERS' LAST WORDS #3

A	B	C	D	E	F	G	H	I	J	K	L	M	N	O	P	Q	R	S	T	U	V	W	X	Y	Z
														P	N								M		

```
'  __ __    P  __ __ __ __ __ __ __    __ __ __    __ __ __ __    __ __ __ __    __ __ X
   B  U     N  O  Y  Y  B  V  J        Y  E  I     L  F  S  I     C  B  G  A     E  I  M

O  __    __ __ __    O  __    O  __ __    O  __ __    __ __ __    __ __ __ __ __ __
P  V     F  X  X     P  R     Z  P  O     D  E  P     E  F  A     F  V  Z  Y  E  B  V  J

__ O    __ O    __ __ __ __    __ __    __ __ __ __    P  __ __ __ __ __ __
Y  P     A  P    D  B  Y  E     U  I     C  B  V  J     N  O  V  B  T  E  I  A

__ __ __ __    __ __    __ O __ __ :    __ O __    __ __ __ __    __ __ __
U  F  G  S     U  Z     D  P  G  A  T    Z  P  O    D  B  X  X     A  B  I

__ __ __ O __ __    __    __ O.
C  I  R  P  G  I     B     A  P
```

- Jake Bird -

KILLERS' LAST WORDS #4

Use the same key for the next two puzzles and find out what food-related puns these killers made before they were executed.

▶▶▶ DO NOT CROSS ◀◀◀   ▶▶▶ STOP ◀◀◀   ▶▶▶ DO NOT CROSS ◀◀◀   ▶▶▶ STOP ◀◀◀   ▶▶▶ DO NOT CROSS ◀◀◀

A	B	C	D	E	F	G	H	I	J	K	L	M	N	O	P	Q	R	S	T	U	V	W	X	Y	Z
				T	I																				

```
_  E  _     F  E  _  _  _  _  _ !                                  F  _  _
E  T  L     I  T  V  V  W  H    E M Q    W J M B S    S E R H    I  M  U

_        E  _  _  _  _  _     E    F  _  _                    '          _  _ _ E  ?
W     E  T  W  K  V  R  X  T    I  M  U    S M F M U U M Q H    A W A T U

F  E  _  _  _     F  _  _  E  .
I  U  T  X  Y  E    I  U  R  T  H
```

- James French -

```
_  E  _  _     _  E  _  _  E  _  E  _ ,    _  _ _     _  E  _
Q  T  V  V    D  T  X  S  V  T  F  T  X    L M B    W U T    W J M B S

_  _     _  _  _  E  _  _     _     _  _  E  _     _  _  _  E  _ .
S  M    Q  R  S  X  T  H  H    W    J  W  G  T  K    W A A T V
```

- George Appel -

KILLERS' LAST MEALS

Match the killer to the last meal they had before their execution.

Black coffee

Timothy McVeigh

Wiener schnitzel, fried potatoes, and a bottle of white wine

Fritz Haarmann

Nothing

William Bonin

A cigar and a cup of Brazilian coffee

Charles Starkweather

Two pints of mint chocolate chip ice cream

Peter Kürten

Boiled eggs, toast, and coffee

H. H. Holmes

Cold cuts

Aileen Wuornos

A dozen deep-fried shrimp, a bucket of KFC original recipe chicken, fries, and a pound of strawberries

Ted Bundy

Shrimp, lobster, a baked potato, strawberry cheesecake, and sweet tea

Danny Rolling

Two pepperoni and sausage pizzas, chocolate ice cream, and three six-packs of Coca-Cola and Pepsi

John Wayne Gacy

HISTORICAL CRIMES

Use the hints below to unscramble the names of these historical criminals.

1. **ITDOYPH MRYA** _____
2. **HTE LYBODO DBESNRE** _____
3. **ETH YLKEL LMYFIA** _____
4. **SARTVNE GRIL ITHOALNARNI** _____
5. **YMRA NNA CNTOOT** _____
6. **KBRUE NDA EHAR** _____
7. **JANE RERINEG** _____
8. **JHON "IEGRTINAELV" OHOJSNN** _____
9. **NJAE NPAPOT** _____
10. **BELEL SGNSNUE** _____
11. **KACJ TEH PRPEIR** _____
12. **EHKRKITEFNIA XEA RRUSDEM** _____
13. **XMAENA FO NWE AENOLRS** _____
14. **DIENEPHL IARELAUL** _____
15. **EHIELTBAZ BHYRAOT** _____

>>> DO NOT CROSS <<< >>> STOP <<< >>> DO NOT CROSS <<< >>> STOP <<< >>> DO NOT CROSS <<<

CLUES!

1. Nickname of a cook, and carrier of a deadly disease, who infected up to 122 people
2. America's first serial killer family
3. Family of serial killers who committed a series of murders from their Kansas tavern in 1887
4. AKA the Austin Axe Murderer, or the Midnight Assassin, unknown killer who murdered eight women in their beds
5. Believed to have killed 11 of her 13 children, and three of her four husbands
6. Famous English graverobbers
7. Young French boy who believed he was a werewolf
8. Killed 300 people of the Crow Tribe of Montana as revenge for his wife's murder
9. Nurse and poisoner who said she derived sexual pleasure from her patients being close to death
10. Wealthy landowner who sourced victims through newspaper personal ads and may have faked her own death
11. Unknown Victorian serial killer working in the Whitechapel area of London
12. Name for March 21, 1922 killing of six victims by an unknown person, who lived in the house with his dead victims for three days after the attacks
13. Unknown killer who promised not to murder anyone who had a jazz band playing in their homes on the night of March 19, 1919
14. New Orleans socialite whose house caught fire, revealing many tortured enslaved people
15. Hungarian noblewoman also known as the Blood Countess

HISTORICAL CRIMES

```
I  S  R  E  D  R  U  M  E  X  A  K  E  F  I  A  K  R  E  T  N  I  H  K
C  U  V  Q  G  G  C  Q  L  X  G  P  N  Z  F  J  L  N  K  J  N  T  P  R
V  X  F  C  R  F  O  W  K  S  N  U  Z  A  J  V  E  H  F  C  G  N  B  S
K  D  Z  K  Q  O  W  F  N  O  T  T  O  C  N  N  A  Y  R  A  M  D  E  W
A  Y  I  O  S  R  E  D  N  E  B  Y  D  O  O  L  B  T  I  R  D  R  D  A
X  E  Z  H  J  S  R  H  R  J  I  Y  R  W  B  X  A  B  J  G  V  H  H  H
E  U  F  R  R  D  S  V  Q  N  B  J  N  V  J  U  F  Q  T  A  Z  E  G  N
M  L  O  S  O  M  X  E  V  X  E  T  S  O  I  J  R  F  N  F  T  J  L  D
A  U  I  M  D  Z  Z  J  N  A  O  T  Z  C  S  V  V  T  M  D  V  T  M  R
N  K  O  Z  X  E  P  C  N  N  Y  A  H  P  I  N  G  K  X  I  E  A  T  E
O  U  W  X  A  X  L  G  F  M  U  J  X  Z  D  I  H  X  D  K  H  U  C  P
F  P  S  O  N  B  R  P  T  A  Y  G  R  G  R  S  T  O  P  I  A  G  E  P
N  W  S  T  S  E  E  S  H  M  I  U  E  L  N  X  T  F  J  W  N  R  K  I
E  A  L  H  N  T  S  T  B  I  A  K  A  L  F  T  V  A  U  N  A  W  N  R
W  G  P  I  R  P  Y  Q  H  Y  N  N  E  N  L  H  C  U  U  H  H  J  D  E
O  E  E  P  A  C  M  P  G  B  N  E  F  L  L  E  W  L  D  L  J  O  A  H
R  R  S  M  O  Q  F  B  H  I  A  G  L  R  L  H  B  N  V  D  E  Z  J  T
L  T  B  Y  W  T  D  P  H  O  W  T  D  A  Q  Y  A  V  T  B  B  D  B  K
E  I  Z  U  G  U  E  I  C  T  I  T  H  L  L  E  F  K  M  I  V  V  O  C
A  X  U  Q  H  P  L  N  M  A  G  D  E  O  K  A  T  A  O  U  V  X  X  A
N  T  I  P  W  A  H  G  A  H  Q  P  M  R  R  Y  U  R  M  M  Y  Z  B  J
S  K  X  S  T  A  F  F  M  J  H  I  U  A  H  Y  G  R  Y  I  W  I  T  S
Q  D  Y  O  S  V  S  W  N  N  A  B  X  G  R  C  N  S  I  C  L  Y  Y  U
X  L  R  Z  G  A  J  U  V  A  F  L  J  I  L  Y  T  U  E  E  K  Y  C  A
```

ELIZABETH BATHORY   **DELPHINE LALAURIE**   **AXEMAN OF NEW ORLEANS**

HINTERKAIFEK AXE MURDERS   **JACK THE RIPPER**   **BELLE GUNNESS**   **JANE TOPPAN**

JOHN JOHNSON   **JEAN GRENIER**   **BURKE AND HARE**   **MARY ANN COTTON**   **KELLY FAMILY**

SERVANT GIRL ANNIHILATOR   **BLOODY BENDERS**   **TYPHOID MARY**

WHAT HAVE YOU LEARNED?

The answer to each of these questions can be found by completing the puzzles in this chapter.

1. Ted Bundy was given steak, eggs, hash browns, and toast for his last meal; what did he end up eating?

_____

2. What creature did Jean Grenier claim to be?

_____

3. What "profession" were Burke and Hare famous for?

_____

4. Fred West once had what seemingly wholesome career?

_____

5. Who wondered if he could hear his own blood rushing from his head after his execution?

_____

6. George Appel's last words made reference to which dessert?

_____

7. Who referenced the movie _Independence Day_ in their last words?

_____

8. What music did the Axeman of New Orleans enjoy?

_____

9. Who were said to be America's first serial killer family?

_____

10. Who killed his cellmate to ensure he would be given the death penalty?

_____

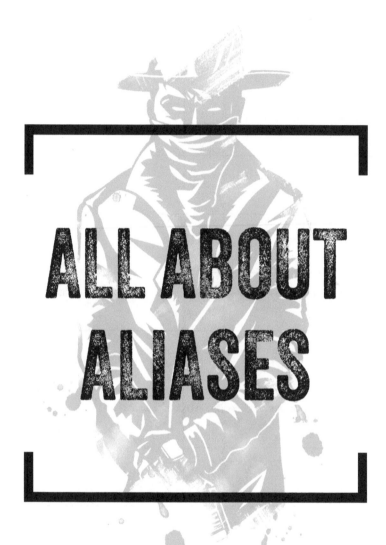

ALL ABOUT ALIASES

KILLER TO ALIAS

1. The Night Stalker	a. Richard Ramirez
2. The Golden State Killer	b. Pedro Alonso López
3. The Butcher of Rostov	c. Gary Ridgway
4. The Giggling Granny	d. Harold Shipman
5. The Little Old Lady Killer	e. John George Haigh
6. The Green River Killer	f. Andrei Chikatilo
7. Doctor Death	g. Peter Sutcliffe
8. Son of Sam	h. Ilse Koch
9. The Co-Ed Killer	i. Ted Kaczynski
10. The Killer Clown	j. Juana Barraza
11. BTK	k. Keith Hunter Jesperson
12. The Acid Bath Murderer	l. Joseph DeAngelo
13. Hell's Belle	m. Richard Chase
14. The Unabomber	n. Ed Kemper
15. The Yorkshire Ripper	o. David Berkowitz
16. The Witch of Buchenwald	p. Nannie Doss
17. The Vampire of Sacramento	q. John Wayne Gacy
18. The Monster of the Andes	r. Alexander Pichushkin
19. The Chessboard Killer	s. Dennis Rader
20. The Happy Face Killer	t. Belle Gunness

MURDER MONIKERS #1

DOWN

1. What the "Co-ed Killer" Ed Kemper told the judge his punishment should be

2. Nickname of Robert Hansen, Alaskan serial killer who abducted women and freed them in the wilderness so he could hunt them for sport

3. New name David Berkowitz gave himself after finding religion in prison

4. Tracking metadata on this outdated piece of technology led to BTK's arrest

5. Nickname of killer caught thanks to evidence provided by his own brother

6. The #1 suspect in the Zodiac Killer case

7. Amount of years Pedro Alonso López "The Monster of the Andes" served in prison

ACROSS

8. Nickname of killer who attempted to cover his tracks by changing his tires, and buying new shoes after every kill

9. Restaurant John Wayne Gacy managed

10. Scottish murderer nicknamed after a holy book

11. What the acronym BTK stood for

12. How "Doctor Death," Harold Shipman, killed his victims

MURDER MONIKERS #2

ACROSS

5. One of The Golden State Killer's other nicknames

6. Famous L.A. hotel where Richard Ramirez "The Night Stalker" stayed

7. Country in which "The Ogre of the Ardennes" killed

8. The accent police believed they were looking for in the "Yorkshire Ripper" case, leading to the actual killer being dismissed as a suspect

DOWN

1. Nickname of Albert DeSalvo, murderer of 13 women in the 1960s

2. Name for the killings committed by South African killer Moses Sithole, based on the name of the towns he committed his crimes

3. What Son of Sam claimed convinced him to kill

4. Group of Hungarian women who mainly murdered abusive husbands

VICTIM COUNT

Rank these 10 killers in order of number of confirmed victims, their age, and the date they were apprehended by police:

A. Joseph DeAngelo

B. Nannie Doss

C. John Wayne Gacy

D. Dennis Rader

E. Andrei Chikatilo

F. David Berkowitz

G. Richard Ramirez

H. Keith Hunter Jesperson

I. Gary Ridgway

J. Juana Barraza

Confirmed Victim Count	Age (Oldest to youngest)	Date Apprehended (Most recent to longest ago)

CREEPY QUOTES #1

Solve these puzzles to reveal some truly creepy quotes by notorious killers.

A	B	C	D	E	F	G	H	I	J	K	L	M	N	O	P	Q	R	S	T	U	V	W	X	Y	Z
			R																						

```
     E                        E                      E
_  _ _     _ _ _ _    _ _ _ _    _ _ _    _ _ _
P  I R     D M Y C    P I Q M W  P I R C  A F M    W R P

  E                                 E
_ _     _ _ _    _ _    _ _ _ _ _ _    _    _ _ _ _ _ _
N R     J D X    Q B    X H M M Q M W  F    J H M R X F Y

                              E     E
_ _ _ _ _ _    _ _ _ _ _ _    _    _ _ _ _ _ _
E F X Y D X    Z Q P I D H P  F    Y Q A R M B R
```

- John Wayne Gacy -

>>> DO NOT CROSS <<< >>> STOP <<< >>> DO NOT CROSS <<< >>> STOP <<< >>> DO NOT CROSS <<<

A	B	C	D	E	F	G	H	I	J	K	L	M	N	O	P	Q	R	S	T	U	V	W	X	Y	Z
							T	O																	

```
        I                          I'     I
_ _ _   _ _ _ _   _ _   _ _   _ _ _ _   _ _   _ _ _ _
K P S   C O I S   K L   Y S   C J M C   O I   U O F S

              H                    H         H
_ _   _ _ _ _   _ _   _ _ _   _ _ _ _   _ _ _   _ _ _
G K   G J U F   G K   T S V   I J G S   T S V   G T S

    H               I                      I
_ _ _ _ _   _ _ _ _   _ _   _ _   _ _ _ _   _
K G T S V   C O I S   K L   Y S   C J M C   O

        H         H         H
_ _ _ _ _   _ _ _ _   _ _ _   _ _ _ _   _ _ _ _ _
Z K P I S V Z T J G   T S V   T S J I   Z K N U I

            I                          I
_ _ _ _   _ _ _ _   _ _   _   _ _ _ _ _ ?
U K K F   U O F S   K P   J   C G O H F
```

- Ed Kemper -

CREEPY QUOTES #2

A	B	C	D	E	F	G	H	I	J	K	L	M	N	O	P	Q	R	S	T	U	V	W	X	Y	Z
F														O											

```
                      A                                      A
__  __  _____  _  ___  _____  __  _
L T  V D  R E H F V  L  M H H  X H N A E H  V H  F

            T
_____  __  _____  _____
N A E H M O  A N  K E Z K L N L B H M  S P L K P

    A   A      T        T       T        A T
_____  ____  ____  _____ .  __
Y E F R Z F C C D  O Z E T  L T O A  O E H H M  F O

      T T       A      A     T
_____  _____  _____  __  ___
N L E M O  O P H E H  F W H F E M  O A  X H  R H S

      A                        T
__  ____  _____  ____  ___
A E  E F L T  R E L W W L T Y  N E A V  O P H

      A           T A ,   A       A  ,  _
_____,  ___  __  _____   _
X E F T K P H M,  X Z O  F M  L  F W W E A F K P  L

      A       T
_____  __  __  _____ .
E H F C L T H  L O  L M  X C A A R
```

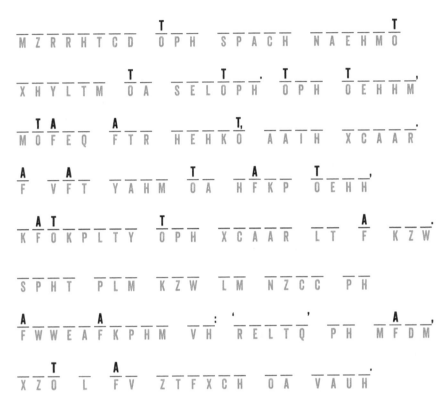

```
     T              _                    T
M Z R R H T C D   O P H   S P A C H   N A E H M O

        T          T     . T     T
X H Y L T M   O A   S E L O P H   O P H   O E H H M ,

   T A       A              T,
M O F E Q   F T R   H E H K O   A A I H   X C A A R .

A       A           T       A       T
F   V F T   Y A H M   O A   H F K P   O E H H ,

   A T             T                         A
K F O K P L T Y   O P H   X C A A R   L T   F   K Z W .

S P H T   P L M   K Z W   L M   N Z C C   P H

A           A               :  '           '         A
F W W E A F K P H M   V H   R E L T Q   P H   M F D M ,

      T       A
X Z O   L   F V   Z T F X C H   O A   V A U H .
```

- John George Haigh -

GRUESOME WORDS

```
O  B  E  Y  S  O  F  O  S  S  G  E  O  O  M  D  A  T  Q  E  Q  X  K  U
A  B  N  E  E  K  K  J  H  X  V  P  N  B  S  A  R  I  P  P  E  R  L  C
R  A  I  D  R  S  B  U  U  T  N  X  K  M  F  O  I  V  R  O  T  C  E  E
H  R  S  L  I  D  A  Y  Y  R  E  H  S  A  L  S  A  O  C  E  I  A  I  M
A  E  S  Q  A  Y  I  S  T  A  P  I  X  H  P  T  K  Y  N  E  K  W  Y  A
F  P  A  Y  L  A  B  I  N  N  A  C  M  Y  F  S  P  M  I  I  E  U  K  N
Y  A  S  J  N  R  Q  B  E  A  S  T  Z  T  G  C  T  U  H  R  A  S  O  K
J  E  S  V  D  D  Y  M  M  I  I  V  H  P  W  F  J  W  E  P  J  C  C  C
S  R  A  H  J  E  S  O  D  M  E  A  O  G  C  K  E  W  E  K  Q  Q  D  I
G  V  F  F  A  Q  T  W  R  A  B  M  X  V  S  C  O  B  O  Q  A  S  P  N
J  W  V  W  L  W  R  B  J  N  Z  P  C  X  I  L  U  Z  Y  S  Y  U  B  J
W  T  O  X  H  M  A  P  T  I  H  I  I  H  F  T  G  V  F  Y  N  T  H  N
A  A  R  S  Z  X  N  N  G  A  T  R  Q  E  C  D  A  K  I  L  L  E  R  K
C  N  G  O  P  Z  G  F  I  C  O  E  F  H  O  I  P  W  O  F  Z  K  P  N
I  W  N  U  W  L  L  D  I  S  H  G  E  Q  R  R  J  R  H  Z  F  U  P  R
N  A  M  I  N  R  E  S  T  B  N  R  H  I  U  C  E  N  X  E  K  V  P  V
C  Q  K  U  H  D  R  T  E  R  C  O  J  F  K  I  F  K  K  K  H  R  J  V
P  B  D  F  T  I  S  J  G  N  E  C  B  E  F  B  J  I  L  K  G  A  J  N
W  F  B  U  M  I  L  H  P  C  K  N  Y  G  S  Z  S  P  Z  A  R  O  N  R
F  E  B  A  M  R  L  A  M  D  T  C  O  V  T  N  Q  Z  U  W  T  Y  B  K
M  G  Q  C  I  Q  G  A  T  O  P  O  F  S  I  Z  U  M  Z  S  W  S  J  I
L  W  C  Y  B  L  O  K  T  O  W  Z  J  P  I  E  E  K  N  V  A  F  N  K
J  Y  M  E  N  D  O  F  O  R  O  E  Q  E  O  T  C  W  M  B  H  G  V
J  W  Y  N  C  Z  F  R  L  N  R  R  Z  B  J  I  P  F  W  P  H  M  U  M
```

BUTCHER   ASSASSIN   REAPER   MANIAC   ANNIHILATOR   MUTILATOR   SNIPER

BEAST   SLASHER   CANNIBAL   STRANGLER   POISONER   KILLER   STALKER

RIPPER   WEREWOLF   VAMPIRE   SERIAL   NICKNAME

ALSO KNOWN AS

```
P A C I D B A T H M U R D E R E R F V D M W A H
O X T Z T B I R W Y I D K U X K V T N D Y U G D
P V S V C A S A T O M T I W E X W I J T N R N S
C C Y S E X W E Y E D H L X P S B D Y T P E A N
L H Q I F U T I Y S U S L O S F I R Y I N L F B
R E K A B R E H C T U B V J G D E T O N J L L R
R P R E P P I R V O T S O R F L H J P E R I A O
E J F Z O J W Y J A J U W P L A Z S O P F K T O
L A Z G K C G W O A S O C I L N O F I J S R E K
L C W D U Y O X L R R X K L N N D Z A R P E M L
I K P D R J Z K T W K C Y U K T F S E O G V H Y
K T W L R E M D X X A S N Q A N W R G R F I T N
E H C C W Y L B Y I E B H I T W E O P J X R A V
C E Q D Z L S L D F Q J K I G D T Z Y R W N E A
A R L U E I Q O I K N C U W R H I Q E X W E D M
F I R Q K C Z C P K Z K C U E E T Z N T F E R P
Y P S O N O F S A M S F M C I S R S V I K R O I
P P E O N S Q T C Q I S L R J P V I T R Y G T R
P E Q R V G K H W I R O E U G Y D K P A N S C E
A R E X U Z H Z D O W P E R G C V Z U P L J O J
H S M I A T R T O N M M A H D R R W L Z E K D W
W X A D R U R M Z S K W H S L D K M F I Q R E V
W M M M Q Z R O J K P Y I M G Y E X I U J F D R
B M Q S Z Y V W T M A E V A Y X R R W I V O L F
```

AUNTY THALLY   **JACK THE RIPPER**   **DOCTOR DEATH**   **HAPPY FACE KILLER**   **METAL FANG**

POGO THE CLOWN   **BROOKLYN VAMPIRE**   **YORKSHIRE RIPPER**   **SON OF SAM**   **NIGHT STALKER**

ACID BATH MURDERER   **ROSTOV RIPPER**   **RED DRESS KILLER**   **MOORS MURDERERS**   **KILL**

TORTURE   **BIND**   **GREEN RIVER KILLER**   **BUTCHER BAKER**   **ZODIAC KILLER**

WORLD MAP

Locate the killing ground of 20 killers.

(1) Zodiac
(San Francisco, California)

(2) ABC Killer
(South Africa)

(3) Jack the Ripper
(London, England)

(4) Ken and Barbie Killers
(Ontario, Canada)

(5) Beasts of Satan
(Italy)

(6) Bible John
(Glasgow, Scotland)

(7) Blood Countess
(Hungary)

(8) BTK
(Kansas, U.S.A.)

(9) Chessboard Killer
(Russia)

(10) Butcher Baker
(Alaska, U.S.A.)

(11) Green River Killer
(Washington State, U.S.A.)

(12) El Chalequero
(Mexico)

(13) Little Petey
(Brazil)

(14) Moors Murderers
(Manchester, England)

(15) Aunty Thally
(Australia)

(16) The Red Dress Killer
(China)

(17) Cyanide Mallika
(India)

(18) Drumstick Killer
(Japan)

(19) Metal Fang
(Kazakhstan)

(20) Ogre of the Ardennes
(France)

YOU CAN CALL ME...

Solve these picture puzzles to reveal some killer aliases!

 + −

 + + − + +

 + − F + − K

+ − M + − S

YOU CAN CALL ME...

[windmill] − [wind] + [walk] + [key] + [can] + [eye]

[father/son ↓] + OFTEN − 10 + [test tube] − PLE

[calendar] + ING + [board game] + [backpack] − T

+ [angry face] − E

ALIASES

Use the word bank below to help you unscramble these killers' nicknames.

1. **NOGRIILA NHTIG SRETAKL** _____
2. **ILNGGGIG NANGRY** _____
3. **DEHRCBSAOS LRIKLE** _____
4. **OTSORV EPRIPR** _____
5. **OSN FO SMA** _____
6. **BNID TRETUOR LKIL** _____
7. **TDRCOO DETAH** _____
8. **AETLM FNAG** _____
9. **RBYOKNLO IAEMPVR** _____
10. **WKALIEUME BANNIACL** _____
11. **ZICDAO LLRIEK** _____
12. **ELBBI HJNO** _____
13. **JCAK TEH IPRERP** _____
14. **NKE DAN IARBEB LILSERK** _____
15. **LLTTEI DLO DLAY RLIEKL** _____
16. **YKISRHROE PPRERI** _____
17. **OBSTON ALGRSNRTE** _____
18. **PAHPY FAEC KLLIRE** _____
19. **NGEER VRIRE ELLRIK** _____
20. **LEKLIR OLWNC** _____

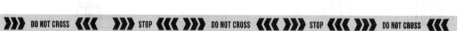

>>> DO NOT CROSS <<< >>> STOP <<< >>> DO NOT CROSS <<< >>> STOP <<< >>> DO NOT CROSS <<<

HINTS!

Each of these killers' aliases appears in the puzzle above.
The remaining four were never caught

Nikolai Dzumagaliev

Joseph DeAngelo

Juana Barraza

Albert DeSalvo

Peter Sutcliffe

Andrei Chikatilo

Paul Bernardo and Karla
Homolka

David Berkowitz

John Wayne Gacy

Nannie Doss

Jeffrey Dahmer

Alexander Pichushkin

Dennis Rader

Gary Ridgway

Albert Fish

Keith Hunter Jesperson

WHAT HAVE YOU LEARNED?

1. What notable children's toys were killers Paul Bernardo and Karla Homolka named after?

    _____

2. In what modern-day country did "Metal Fang" do his killings?

    _____

3. What was another nickname given to The Golden State Killer?

    _____

4. Where did the Beasts of Satan operate?

    _____

5. Who spoke of dreaming about a forest dripping in blood?

    _____

6. Who was caught thanks to metadata from a floppy disk he sent to the police?

    _____

7. Why was the Yorkshire Ripper Peter Sutcliffe dismissed by police several times?

    _____

8. Duan Guocheng only killed women wearing what color?

    _____

9. What did John Wayne Gacy say was the only thing he could be charged for?

    _____

10. Son of Sam changed his name to Son of What after finding religion in prison?

    _____

KILLER DUOS

PARTNERS IN CRIME

Match the killer to their partner in crime.

1. Fred		a. Debra
2. Ronald		b. Lee Boyd
3. Karla		c. Michael Bear
4. Ian		d. Michel
5. Henry		e. Maria
6. David		f. Clyde
7. Dean		g. Rose
8. Kenneth		h. Myra
9. Bonnie		i. Ottis
10. Christine		j. Reginald
11. Leonard		k. Doug
12. Carol		l. Faye
13. Suzan		m. Angelo
14. Ray		n. Dylan
15. Delfina		o. Elmer
16. John Allen		p. Catherine
17. Eric		q. Paul
18. Alton		r. Lea
19. Monique		s. Charles

PAIRS OF PERIL

```
V  B  V  M  O  O  R  S  M  U  R  D  E  R  E  R  S  Z  K  Z  R  P  L  X
I  L  S  S  P  K  J  Q  Y  S  T  S  C  P  I  O  P  T  K  E  B  Q  Q  X
R  Q  Y  U  E  P  P  E  F  M  I  M  X  U  E  D  A  E  I  L  O  F  D  Y
G  N  D  B  N  S  U  X  U  H  Q  A  J  K  N  X  P  C  K  K  B  A  A  H
I  C  A  K  G  S  H  I  L  L  S  I  D  E  S  T  R  A  N  G  L  E  R  S
N  I  V  G  S  Q  E  N  P  M  B  J  Q  Y  T  V  G  K  R  S  O  X  A  U
H  C  I  N  X  P  N  T  R  A  L  O  T  Z  B  X  E  W  N  N  W  O  P  E
U  Z  D  R  U  O  O  V  S  R  P  K  N  O  R  N  K  V  P  I  V  X  N  M
N  J  A  B  J  M  I  U  W  T  O  I  A  N  A  T  T  S  G  W  P  W  U  W
T  Z  N  L  X  Q  S  F  J  C  R  X  N  N  I  U  G  E  B  T  V  W  Q  V
E  U  D  Z  L  U  S  S  R  X  H  I  D  S  S  E  G  Y  N  Y  P  Q  N  X
R  J  C  H  B  T  E  I  D  K  D  B  P  J  I  A  A  G  W  A  O  Y  P  O
S  D  A  H  W  A  F  R  E  D  A  N  D  R  O  S  E  N  V  R  B  E  D  Q
H  B  T  Y  S  M  N  A  F  R  H  P  R  H  S  U  T  R  D  K  A  F  N  I
B  X  H  K  A  O  O  B  B  G  C  E  M  I  B  C  U  E  K  C  D  Y  Q  K
W  Z  E  D  I  P  C  I  S  A  N  W  U  L  S  A  S  X  R  S  L  G  F  X
E  B  R  E  L  H  E  J  V  G  H  E  V  R  M  N  N  X  L  S  A  Y  Q  D
D  F  I  X  A  S  F  V  A  L  K  Y  S  X  P  D  T  E  V  T  N  L  D  C
M  A  N  W  M  G  N  L  X  K  O  H  D  K  K  Y  C  B  T  Z  D  R  Z  E
Z  R  E  Y  N  N  M  R  E  G  V  O  S  Q  M  M  U  L  O  A  S  P  K  G
B  M  L  O  N  E  L  Y  H  E  A  R  T  S  E  A  O  P  X  O  B  Y  O  T
O  Z  O  Z  D  M  L  T  H  G  B  U  Y  Z  T  N  A  H  W  G  Y  S  L  E
Z  G  I  G  Y  C  Y  E  R  J  T  U  H  T  X  S  M  Q  T  C  X  Z  R  W
Y  A  J  D  H  U  Q  I  X  H  T  L  X  L  P  V  C  P  P  P  V  M  L  G
```

VIRGIN HUNTERS   BADLANDS   TOYBOX   SUNSET STRIP   DAVID AND CATHERINE   PAPIN SISTERS

KRAY TWINS   LONELY HEARTS   FRED AND ROSE   BONNIE AND CLYDE   HILLSIDE STRANGLERS

CONFESSION   KEN AND BARBIE   FOLIE A DEUX   CANDYMAN   MOORS MURDERERS

VICTIM COUNT

Rank these 10 killers in order of number of confirmed victims, their age, and the date they were apprehended by police

A. Kenneth Bianchi and Angelo Buono

B. Ian Brady and Myra Hindley

C. Paul Bernardo and Karla Homolka

D. Dean Corll and Elmer Wayne Henley

E. David and Catherine Birnie

F. John Allen Muhammad and Lee Boyd Malvo

G. Gonzalez Sisters

H. Charles Starkweather and Caril Ann Fugate

I. Bonnie Parker and Clyde Barrow

J. Christine and Lea Papin

Confirmed Victim Count	Date Apprehended (Most recent to longest ago)

MURDEROUS MULTIPLES #1

DOWN

1. With "Killers," nickname of Martha Beck and Raymond Fernandez
2. Nickname for cousin killers Kenneth Bianchi and Angelo Buono Jr
3. Crimes committed by David and Catherine Birnie
5. Killers who murdered their own daughter and buried her in their yard
8. Famous entertainer the Kray Twins hired to sing for their mother

ACROSS

4. Victorian practice Sarah and John Makin used to gain access to victims
6. Item Ray and Faye Copeland made out of their victims' clothes
7. Moor where Myra Hindley and Ian Brady committed their murders
9. Nickname of Dean Corll
10. Psychological phenomenon seen in the Papin Sisters case
11. Killing partner of "Confession Killer" Henry Lee Lucas
12. Famous 1930s outlaw couple
13. Dolls Paul Bernardo and Karla Homolka were compared to
14. App used by Bailey Boswell and Aubrey Trail to find their victim

MURDEROUS MULTIPLES #2

DOWN

1. What Suzan and James Carson called themselves

2. Nickname of Charles Starkweather and Caril Ann Fugate

3. Age of Christine Paolilla when she murdered four people with boyfriend Christopher Lee

4. Brothel run by Delfina and María de Jesús González

5. Nickname of Monique Olivier and Michel Fourniret, based on the victims they would choose

6. Nickname of Cindy Hendy's boyfriend David Parker Ray, who she kidnapped victims for

10. Where Eric Harris and Dylan Klebold carried out their 1999 mass shooting

11. Mountain range where Leonard Lake and Charles Ng committed their murders

13. Family member of Karla's who Paul Bernardo and Karla Homolka murdered

ACROSS

7. Potential victim let go by The Hillside Stranglers "out of respect" for her famous father

8. University of Chicago students who committed "the crime of the century" as an attempt to demonstrate their superior intellect

9. Nickname of John Allen Muhammed and Lee Boyd Malvo

12. With "Killers," L.A.-based nickname of Carol Bundy and Doug Clark

CREEPY QUOTES

Solve this cryptogram to see what disturbing things The Confession Killer said about his victims and other people like him.

A	B	C	D	E	F	G	H	I	J	K	L	M	N	O	P	Q	R	S	T	U	V	W	X	Y	Z
								K														A			

```
__  __I__I_  ____  __I_  ___W  W__  W__
V Z  U K P R K V T  S I U I H  J S I A  A O X R  A X T

__I__  __  _____  __  ____.  I'__  ___
F B K S F  R B  O X M M I S  R B  R O I V  K U I  O X N

_____I_,  __I_I___,  ____I_____
T O B B R K S F  J S K E K S F T  T R H X S F C Y X R K B S T

_____I_,  I'__  _____I_I____  I_
W I X R K S F T  X S N  K U I  M X H R K P K M X R I N  K S

_____  _I_I_I___  __  _____.  __
X P R C X Y  P H C P K E K Q K B S T  B E  O C V X S T  X Y

_____  ___  _____  _____,
Y X P H B T T  R O I  P B C S R H Z  R O I H I T

_____  ____  I_  __  W__  ___  ___
M I B M Y I  G C T R  Y K J I  V I  A O B  T I R  B C R

__  _____  I__.
R B  N I T R H B Z  Y K E I
```

- Henry Lee Lucas -

WHAT HAVE YOU LEARNED?

1. What was the name of the Victorian practice that was essentially a precursor to the foster care system and allowed killers like Sarah and John Makin to get their hands on many victims?

_____

2. What biblical killing method did Henry Lee Lucas say he had participated in?

_____

3. Dean Corll shares his sweet-sounding nickname with which iconic horror movie villain?

_____

4. The Moorhouse Murders were committed by which killer couple?

_____

5. The Moors Murders were committed by which other killer couple?

_____

6. Which killer duo murdered one of the members' sisters?

_____

7. Which killer duo murdered their own daughter?

_____

8. Leopold and Loeb committed what was then known as the "crime of the century" in which U.S city?

_____

9. The Sierra Nevada Mountains were the site of the murders by which killer duo?

_____

10. Which famous actor's daughter was spared by the hillside stranglers, allegedly "out of respect" but likely to avoid the press that would come with the killing?

_____

FEMALE KILLERS

FEMME FATALE

Each line below houses the name of a famous female killer. How many can you unscramble?

1. AENLEI UOWRNSO _____

2. LELEB GESUNSN _____

3. EVERLYEB LLTIAT _____

4. DENIA DWNSO _____

5. LAEMAI ERDY _____

6. AMRY YHNDLEI _____

7. EORS STEW _____

8. ARLKA HMLAKOO _____

9. IDEEHLNP LAIERAUL _____

10. EIALEHBZT ORBHTYA _____

11. OHATOERD NETPUE _____

12. ANAJU BARZARA _____

13. ENIANN OSSD _____

14. LZEZII NDOERB _____

15. ILVANAI FREHIS _____

16. UYJD OOUBANEN _____

17. YYSPG RSOE BDRCLANAH _____

18. RSAA NJEA RMEOO _____

19. TREUAGMERI AMERI AILBTER _____

20. NAEJ NPOTAP _____

FEMALE KILLERS

```
Q L Z R D P T R B H O G G B K M T H H O Q U W B
T N L Z K R J B B E J T F P K Q B T U Y O Z E F
N X T B C M A F M I V K R T G U X A I J O L Q V
C J E F A Z N H H A T E N Q Q O T K U L L Z V I
U A D H G O G X C H M O R U X L Z Z U E S O S T
T N C I J J I Y F B N J E M L L T Y O G R Q L R W
O E C N D J G O V C A P L Y E U X U X L I Q U U
V T R O S E W E S T N L T I C Y N Q M V I D F U
G O H D G K I C J Y P E B O A N A D R I G W E N
K P V X K U M R T E Y M F E E D O L A K A F T E
W P A O A A Y C U J A Q F S S R Y G L Z G I R D
L A N I R L Z E J A U N S B O O G E H I H N F R
O N M R L U P A L K L D S T V M R T R R T Z G O
H B X V A A Z W R D M A H N M D S Y Y I M T U B
T N D V H M R L H R N E L K W M C O S P S K F E
Q C N Z O I X C P H A I D E P O A N F P D H F I
I X D C M W P E D P K B H G N Z D W T W Y A S Z
M N Z B O U A N U G R V A A T I Z E Z C X G M Z
L G C V L A I E Y I Y A D N R A H P N A E Q M I
W Y F C K O N B M U N O F R A Y M P V A N L A L
V B F Y A T R D V O L X X H U M M L S I X S F
V E D B E F R X Q Y F G I B F Y J K J E F D W N
X S M N Q O A I L E E N W U O R N O S F D T R X
Y W K L V I H Q O O F M N A N N I E D O S S L J
```

AMELIA DYER   **JANE TOPPAN**   **GYPSY ROSE BLANCHARD**   **DIANE DOWNS**   **LIZZIE BORDEN**

NANNIE DOSS   **ROSE WEST**   **MYRA HINDLEY**   **BEVERLEY ALLITT**   **DOROTHEA PUENTE**

AILEEN WUORNOS   **KARLA HOMOLKA**   **BELLE GUNNESS**   **JUANA BARRAZA**   **DELPHINE LALAURIE**

VICTIM COUNT

Rank these 10 killers in order of number of confirmed victims, their age, and the date they were apprehended by police (Note: two were never caught!).

A. Aileen Wournos

B. Juana Barraza

C. Nannie Doss

D. Elizabeth Báthory

E. Dorothea Puente

F. Belle Gunness

G. Jane Toppan

H. Delphine LaLaurie

I. Beverley Allitt

J. Amelia Dyer

Potential Victim Count	Age (Oldest to youngest)	Date Apprehended (Most recent to longest ago)

LETHAL LADIES #1

DOWN

1. Hygiene item Italian killer Leonarda Cianciulli turned her victims' bodies into
3. Profession of Mexican serial killer Juana Barraza
4. Partner of Bernardo, known as The Most Hated Woman in Canada
8. How Belle Gunness found most of her victims
9. Most common motive for female killers
11. Age Mary Bell was when she committed two murders
12. Patricia Krenwinkel was a member of this famous "family"

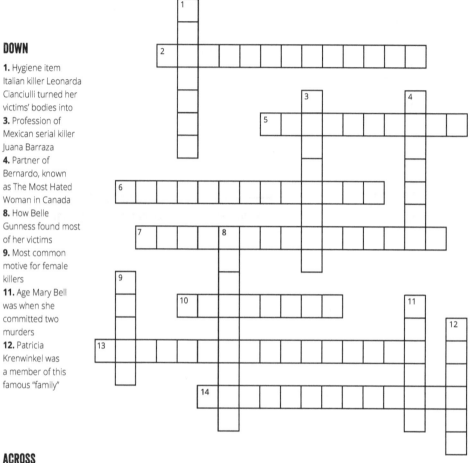

ACROSS

2. First American female serial killer
5. U.S. President Sara Jane Moore attempted to assassinate
6. Woman believed to be Britain's first female serial killer
7. Movie Aileen Wuornos referenced in her last words
10. Killing partner of husband Fred who killed her own daughter
13. New Orleans socialite who is said to have escaped to France once her crimes were uncovered
14. Nickname of Hungarian killer who could have been the inspiration for the urban legend Bloody Mary

LETHAL LADIES #2

DOWN

1. Nickname of Mexican sisters and brothel owners who ran Rancho El Ángel

2. Woman who murdered two husbands, and her own son, by poisoning their meals over a period of several years

4. Partner of Ian Brady

5. Killer who ran a boarding house in Sacramento and preyed on her tenants

6. Karla Faye Tucker's weapon of choice during her 1983 murders

7. Item Lyda Southard used to distill arsenic

ACROSS

3. Jean Lee was the last woman to be executed in this country

8. One of only two women serving a life sentence in England; responsible for the Peterborough Ditch Murders

9. Method many female killers use to murder their victims

10. Drug Amelia Dyer alleged used to kill victims

CREEPY QUOTES

Solve these puzzles to find out what two famous **female** killers said about why they killed.

A	B	C	D	E	F	G	H	I	J	K	L	M	N	O	P	Q	R	S	T	U	V	W	X	Y	Z
				F											L										

```
_ _ _ _   _ _   _ _   _ _ _ _ _ _ :   _ _   _ _ E
H T P H   A X   O W   P O I A H A M C   H M   T P Q F
```

```
_ _ _ _ _ E   _ _ _ _ E   P E _ P _ E   _ _ _ _   _ _ _
S A D D F B   O M Y F   L F M L D F   H T P C   P C W
```

```
_ _ _   _ _   _ _ _ _   _ _ _   _ _ _   E _ E _   _ _ _ E
O P C   M Y   N M O P C   N T M   T P X   F Q F Y   D A Q F B
```

- Jane Toppan -

```
_ _   _ _ E   _ _ _ _   _ _ _ _ _   _ _   _ _ _ _ _ _
H M   O F   H T A X   N M Y D B   A X   C M H T A C U
```

```
_ _ _   E _ _ _ ,   _ _ _   _ _   _ _ _   E _ _ _   _ _ _ _
I R H   F Q A D   P C B   O W   M N C   F Q A D   Z R X H
```

```
_ _ P P E _ E _   _ _   _ _ _ _   _ _ _ E   _ _ '   _ _ E   _ _
T P L L F C B   H M   J M O F   M R H   J P R X F   M E
```

```
_ _ E   _ _ _ _ _ _ _ _ _ _   _ E   _ _ _ _   _
H T F   J A Y J R O X H P C J F X   M E   N T P H   A
```

```
_ _ _   _ _ _ _ _
N P X   B M A C U
```

- Aileen Wuornos -

WHAT HAVE YOU LEARNED?

1. Which two female killers mentioned in this section were never apprehended?

_____

2. Who was the first American female serial killer?

_____

3. From what did Lyda Southard derive the poison she used to kill four of her husbands?

_____

4. What is the most common motive for female killers?

_____

5. What was Jane Toppan's life goal?

_____

6. How old was Mary Bell when she committed her murders?

_____

7. What is a common way female killers murder?

_____

8. Who could have been the inspiration for the urban legend Bloody Mary?

_____

9. Gerald Ford was the target of which would-be assassin?

_____

10. What establishment did Dorothea Puente run, in order to lure in victims?

_____

CELEBRITY AND POP CULTURE

ASSASSINS

Match the celebrity to their assassin.

1. **Abraham Lincoln**		a. Leon Czolgosz
2. **John F. Kennedy**		b. James Earl Ray
3. **Robert Kennedy**		c. Ramón Mercader
4. **Archduke Franz Ferdinand**		d. John Wilkes Booth
5. **Martin Luther King**		e. Satwant Singh and Beant Singh
6. **Mohandas Gandhi**		f. Jack Ruby
7. **William McKinley**		g. Yolanda Saldivar
8. **John Lennon**		h. Gavrilo Princip
9. **Gianni Versace**		i. Yigal Amir
10. **Lee Harvey Oswald**		j. Sirhan Sirhan
11. **Leon Trotsky**		k. Andrew Cunanan
12. **George Moscone and Harvey Milk**		l. Lee Harvey Oswald
13. **Medgar Evers**		m. Dan White
14. **George Brown**		n. George Bennett
15. **Selena Quintanilla-Pérez**		o. The Nation of Islam Members
16. **Indira Gandhi**		p. Hitman hired by his wife
17. **Julius Caesar**		q. Mark David Chapman
18. **Malcolm X**		r. Nathurum Godse
19. **Yitzhak Rabin**		s. Byron De La Beckwith
20. **Maurizio Gucci**		t. Marcus Brutus & others

FAMED FATALITIES #1

DOWN

1. Nickname of Olympian Vladimir Sabich who was shot and killed by girlfriend, French singer Claudine Longet
2. Famous podcast about the Adnan Syed case
3. Soul singer murdered under mysterious circumstances in 1964
4. Margaret Atwood book based on the controversial real-life story of Grace Marks
5. Music producer who killed actress and model Lana Clarkson in 2003
7. Position played by New England Patriot Aaron Hernandez before his arrest for murder
8. Woman killed by Sex Pistols bassist Sid Vicious
9. Athlete and defendant of a sensational 1995 trial

ACROSS

6. Star of *SNL* and *The Simpsons* murdered by his wife in 1998
10. Famous American boxing promoter convicted of manslaughter in 1967
11. Organization that kidnapped Patty Hearst
12. Actress murdered by the Manson Family
13. Movie premiere that publicist Ronni Chasen had been to the night she was killed

FAMED FATALITIES #2

DOWN

1. Netflix docuseries about Henry Lee Lucas

2. TV game show won by serial killer Rodney Alcala

4. City where Tupac Shakur was murdered

6. Canadian professional wrestler who killed his wife and son, then hanged himself

8. City where Biggie Smalls was murdered (abbrev.)

ACROSS

3. Famous fashion designer, and last victim of Andrew Cunanan

5. Iconic 1973 horror movie in which possible serial killer Paul Bateson made an appearance

7. *West Side Story* actress who died under mysterious circumstances

9. Killer who Charles Dickens based the character Mademoiselle Hortense in *Bleak House* on

10. *Poltergeist* actress murdered by her boyfriend in 1982

11. Sensational docuseries about the death of Kathleen Peterson and the subsequent trial of her husband Michael

12. Writer of *Naked Lunch* who accidentally shot and killed his wife during a drunken game of "William Tell"

MURDER BOOKS

Match the book to the killer it is about.

1. *I'll Be Gone in the Dark*

2. *The Stranger Beside Me*

3. *Helter Skelter*

4. *The Devil in the White City*

5. *American Predator*

6. *Vulgar Favors*

7. *Hell's Princess*

8. *A Serial Killer's Daughter*

9. *A Father's Story*

10. *The Night Stalker*

a. Belle Gunness

b. Ted Bundy

c. The Golden State Killer

d. Andrew Cunanan

e. H. H. Holmes

f. Richard Ramirez

g. Dennis Rader "BTK"

h. Charles Manson

i. Israel Keyes

j. Jeffrey Dahmer

CRIME AND JUSTICE QUOTES #1

Use the key below to find out what OJ Simpson had to say about justice and reveal the most famous quote of his sensational trial.

A	B	C	D	E	F	G	H	I	J	K	L	M	N	O	P	Q	R	S	T	U	V	W	X	Y	Z
					P								K												

```
__  _____  O_   O__   __   ___
W I  E U F J W S E   X K D   O F N   E T   U D S G
```

```
_____  __  O__   ___   F F O __
Z D T N W S F   E T   X K D   S E I   E P P K J H
```

- OJ Simpson -

```
_F  __  O_'_  F__  O_  ____
W P  W N  H K F T I N  P W N  X K D  U D T N
```

```
_____
E S B D W N
```

- Johnny Cochran -

CRIME AND JUSTICE QUOTES #2

Use this key to discover what prosecutor Marcia Clark had to say about how some people's true crime obsession developed during the OJ Simpson trial.

A	B	C	D	E	F	G	H	I	J	K	L	M	N	O	P	Q	R	S	T	U	V	W	X	Y	Z
								Z							R										

```
      I
I T F P    D T F    D M Z L Q    U F Y L P'    L Q Q    X B    D T F

                        I
P F D I X M G W    I F M F    Y F D D Z P Y    D T F W F

      -     I
T L D F    K L Z Q    Q F D D F M W    U F N L J W F

P     P    '         P         P                           I
R F X R Q F W    W X L R    X R F M L W    I F M F    U F Z P Y

I              P                        I   P
Z P D F M M J R D F S    B X M    D T F    W Z K R W X P

    I                      ...  P     P              I
D M Z L Q    U J D    D T F P    R F X R Q F    I T X    Q Z G F

          P    P
S W X L R    X R F M L W    Y X D    L S S Z N D F S    D X

          I   P              I
D T F    W Z K R W X P    D M Z L Q    L P S    D T F O    Y X D

               P                           I   P
M F L Q Q O    J R W F D    I T F P    D T F    W Z K R W X P

      I
D M Z L Q    I L W    X A F M
```

- Marcia Clark -

CELEBRITIES

Unscramble each clue below to reveal a famous person who has committed a crime.

1. **JO OINMPSS** _____

2. **NROAA RNNEEAZHD** _____

3. **IPHL POSCETR** _____

4. **DIS USOIIVC** _____

5. **HYNNJO WEILS** _____

6. **EUSG NKGTHI** _____

7. **ODG EHT TBYONU UNRTEH** _____

8. **LCMIAHE CEAJ** _____

9. **ONYDER LLCAAA** _____

10. **NOD NGKI** _____

11. **CHSRI IONETB** _____

12. **NUEAIDLC TLENOG** _____

13. **LILWMAI .S BOHUGRUSR** _____

14. **ONOPS GDGO** _____

15. **EBORRT BALEK** _____

NOTORIOUS CASES

```
R  S  Y  R  U  T  N  E  C  E  H  T  F  O  L  A  I  R  T  W  B  Q  R  L
U  B  A  R  R  Y  C  A  B  D  I  Q  S  S  S  P  T  K  Q  I  M  M  A  E
B  U  J  H  T  R  Z  I  I  Y  T  L  C  S  A  D  V  E  O  D  X  G  B  W
I  F  K  F  R  I  B  O  E  R  P  X  K  E  E  S  T  G  D  G  D  R  V  S
G  O  N  E  V  F  L  H  P  A  D  A  S  J  H  R  R  L  Y  T  L  O  H  N
H  M  G  Y  Q  B  L  A  Z  T  U  D  E  O  U  A  P  L  D  H  W  V  K  O
C  Q  G  C  A  W  P  Q  V  N  D  R  M  E  P  P  X  A  P  M  K  Y  P  A
U  V  H  T  A  A  Y  T  C  E  Z  W  C  H  U  R  S  L  C  P  E  D  Z  U
F  S  N  O  R  C  X  B  L  M  Q  X  Y  R  B  R  V  L  I  F  U  C  J  T
A  C  Z  A  L  H  D  J  Q  U  D  L  F  U  V  U  W  E  U  Y  Z  O  F  H
M  B  Z  F  L  L  V  E  R  C  S  C  A  N  D  A  L  T  T  G  Z  L  Y  Q
E  Z  B  S  X  A  Y  O  E  O  I  K  O  Q  G  Z  V  T  X  G  O  O  O  N
I  B  M  W  C  T  N  W  A  D  U  Z  N  Q  J  T  B  U  O  X  N  Y  R  F
L  E  N  A  C  D  K  O  O  V  E  U  R  E  B  L  S  A  D  A  C  E  D  C
G  F  A  Y  O  Y  C  O  I  O  N  F  A  P  W  S  L  A  Q  F  M  D  R  U
N  I  C  U  E  X  A  B  W  T  D  Q  Q  H  N  S  S  L  C  A  T  I  J  C
I  O  J  J  I  T  W  S  C  C  A  H  Z  V  N  B  R  R  O  D  M  A  O  V
K  F  D  G  R  J  M  E  W  G  I  S  M  H  I  H  D  L  A  E  O  H  L  D
C  D  S  Z  Z  E  K  S  Y  I  E  E  N  O  Y  J  C  Q  S  T  S  P  Q  E
O  A  E  E  E  U  M  S  T  B  V  G  P  E  L  H  G  N  Z  N  S  W  L  V
H  W  C  X  B  T  Q  E  R  X  Q  I  R  J  S  N  R  N  X  X  H  M  C  S
S  S  H  J  R  J  A  D  Z  R  C  P  L  F  L  T  C  I  S  O  W  J  O  Y
B  N  O  I  T  A  N  I  S  S  A  S  S  A  J  M  N  X  S  R  S  O  A  R
O  T  L  P  N  R  P  M  X  W  R  C  E  L  E  B  R  I  T  Y  P  B  D  O
```

TRIAL OF THE CENTURY   PRESS   BIOGRAPHY   BIOPIC   PODCAST   SCANDAL
SENSATIONAL   SHOCKING   PAPARAZZI   TELL-ALL   ASSASSINATION   TABLOID   DOCUMENTARY
CRIME   NEWS   STARS   OBSESSED   HOLLYWOOD   FAME   CELEBRITY

MURDER MOVIES/DOCUSERIES

Match the movie or documentary to the killer it is about.

1. *Don't F*** With Cats*

2. *Monster*

3. *Extremely Wicked, Shockingly Evil, and Vile*

4. *The Staircase*

5. *The Confession Killer*

6. *Out of the Darkness*

7. *Citizen X*

8. *The Gray Man*

9. *The Pig Farm*

10. *Making a Murderer*

11. *Mommy Dead and Dearest*

12. *Tiger King*

13. *The Raincoat Killer*

14. *The Craigslist Killer*

15. *The Honeymoon Killers*

16. *The Snowtown Murders*

17. *Wolf Creek*

18. *Scream*

19. *Memories of a Murderer*

20. *The Ripper*

a. Bunting/Wagner/Vlassakis

b. Andrei Chikatilo

c. David Berkowitz

d. Joseph Maldonado

e. Steven Avery

f. Ted Bundy

g. Philip Markoff

h. Dennis Nilsen

i. Aileen Wuornos

j. Henry Lee Lucas

k. Raymond Fernandez/Martha Beck

l. Peter Sutcliffe

m. Luka Magnotta

n. Michael Peterson

o. Danny Rolling

p. Yoo Young-chul

q. Robert Pickton

r. Ivan Milat

s. Gypsy Rose Blanchard

t. Albert Fish

CRIME SONGS

Match the song to its true crime subject.

1. "Suffer Little Children" - The Smiths

2. "I Just Shot John Lennon" - The Cranberries

3. "Deep Red Bells" - Neko Case

4. "I Don't Like Mondays" - Boomtown Rats

5. "Four Walls" - Bastille

6. "Polly" - Nirvana

7. "Mr. Garfield" - Johnny Cash

8. "Stack O' Lee" - Mississippi John Hurt

9. "Jenny Was a Friend of Mine" - The Killers

10. "Where Is She?" - The Killers

11. "Nebraska" - Bruce Springstein

12. "Wrong 'Em Boyo" - The Clash

13. "Son of Sam" - Dead Boys

14. "The Tower" - Insane Clown Posse

15. "Cassie" - Flyleaf

16. "Death Valley '69" - Sonic Youth

17. "Darkness" - Eminem

18. "Let Him Dangle" - Elvis Costello

19. "Skinned" - Blind Melon

20. "Bullet" - The Misfits

a. Brenda Spencer

b. Lee Shelton

c. Stephen Paddock

d. Ed Gein

e. JFK Assassination

f. Robert Chambers

g. Charles Whitman

h. David Berkowitz

i. Gerald Friend

j. The Moors Murders

k. Stagger Lee

l. Mark David Chapman

m. Charles Starkweather

n. Gary Ridgway

o. Manson Family

p. Derek Bentley

q. Charles Guiteau

r. Luke Mitchel

s. Dick Hickock and Perry Smith

t. Columbine Shooting

WHAT HAVE YOU LEARNED?

1. Who is "I Don't Like Mondays" by The Boomtown Rats about?

2. What reason did Marcia Clark give for why people disliked the OJ Simpson trial being televised?

3. The father of which infamous American killer wrote a memoir about his life?

4. The iconic horror movie *Scream* was largely inspired by what real-life killer?

5. Before he was apprehended, killer Paul Bateson appeared in which horror film?

6. Which famous assassin was himself assassinated before he could be charged with his crime?

7. Who murdered comedian Phil Hartman?

8. Who was the last victim of spree killer Andrew Cunanan?

9. What was the most famous quote to come out of the OJ Simpson trial?

10. Who was Charles Dickens' character Mademoiselle Hortense based on?

PARANORMAL TWIST

WICKED WORDS

Solve this puzzle to find out what a Salem Witch Trial **victim** had to say to her persecutors.

A	B	C	D	E	F	G	H	I	J	K	L	M	N	O	P	Q	R	S	T	U	V	W	X	Y	Z
										U				J											

```
_ O _    _ L _ .    _ _    _ O _ O _ _
D J R    Q L T    Q    U Y Q L    Y    Q I    B J    I J L T    Q

_ _ _ _ _    _ _ _ _    _ O _    _ _ _    _    _ _ _ _ _ _    _ _ _
X Y W Z A    W A Q B    D J R    Q L T    Q    X Y G Q L N    Q B N

_ _    _ O _    _ _ _ _    _ _ _ _    _ _    _ L _ _    _ O _
Y K    D J R    W Q F T    Q X Q D    I D    U Y K T    P J N

_ _ L L    _ _ _ _    _ O _    _ L O O _    _ O    _ _ _ _ _
X Y U U    P Y S T    D J R    C U J J N    W J    N L Y B F
```

- Sarah Good -

MYSTERIOUS HAPPENINGS # 1

DOWN

1. American city known for accusing as many as 200 people of being witches
2. The entity that 12-year-olds Anissa Weier and Morgan Geyser were attempting to please when they stabbed their friend, Payton Leutner
3. In 1804 Francis Smith shot bricklayer Thomas Millwood believing him to be this paranormal creature

ACROSS

4. Creature some suspect Countess Elizabeth Báthory may have been
5. Killer who claimed he was convinced to murder by his neighbour's possessed dog
6. Murdered woman who allegedly solved her own case by possessing the body of her friend and implicating her murderer
7. Name for the sensationalized, unsupported claims of ritual abuse prevalent in 1980s America
8. Location Jack the Ripper said he was writing from in a letter to the head of the Whitechapel Vigilance Committee
9. Name of Missy Lutz' invisible demonic friend in the Amityville Horror haunting
10. Symbol Richard Ramirez left behind at a crime scene and proudly displayed in his court appearances

MYSTERIOUS HAPPENINGS # 2

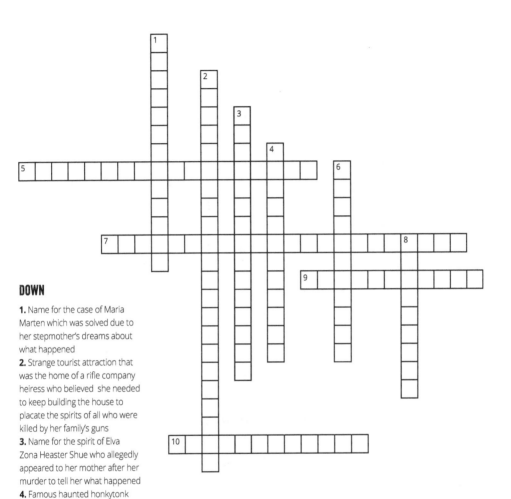

DOWN

1. Name for the case of Maria Marten which was solved due to her stepmother's dreams about what happened

2. Strange tourist attraction that was the home of a rifle company heiress who believed she needed to keep building the house to placate the spirits of all who were killed by her family's guns

3. Name for the spirit of Elva Zona Heaster Shue who allegedly appeared to her mother after her murder to tell her what happened

4. Famous haunted honkytonk in Kentucky that was the site of many accidental deaths and suicides

6. Haunted inn and restaurant in St. Louis that was originally a home where four members of the same family died

8. Restaurant in Oregon, Illinois said to be haunted by the ghost of unsolved murder victim Mary Jane Reed

ACROSS

5. Another name for the Arne Cheyenne Johnson case; the first case in American history to attempt to use demonic possession as a defense

7. Legal drama/horror film based on the alleged possession and eventual death of Anneliese Michel

9. Also called The White Witch, this murderer's spirit is allegedly trapped in the Rose Hall Plantation in Montego Bay, Jamaica

10. Penitentiary in Philadelphia that banned prisoners and guards from speaking, thought to be one of the most haunted prisons in America

WEIRD THINGS

```
S T S O H G H F C C V J O N B I T T F N J X D I
I A O B O Q M I K U E F V U G J T H Q Z S K I Q
L K P V S G B F X O L B H J I I S M Y S H Q A S
W U L J W S Z L I T V E T P N M T M J P U M V R
V L Z C N C L R R Y Y A E C D S K M L H A D C Q
K I E A A V I V O I F N J P S W W K V T T M Y B
K X F Q C Q S N L R I S P L N Q I J F S S J T O
W C X T V B Z D A T R C Z N O F M K Z E A M P D
E S O X Y Q P D E P K O E C M I S R L H P A Q P
O I T D V N N N K V C T H F E G I E Q C Y S I T
E E H I L U T S V R I I M P D L C E S T P R Q H
X V I G R I Z K C U T L N H P R R K Y I E N O S
M Q W D A I B F K B W K X A K U O R L W E P N M
M R Z R Z U P W S A Q B O K T G X B G P R G S G
U M Y V K T S S U L U T H V A A E L P V C A E Q
L L V M U N V T E Q C A C F Q P S L L Z Z E M H
Y P Z W P F F C O L U O S A U U N O D V H R H T
S R M F A Z I Z O N T M N V E J U Y I X R W A B
A O M Q N C E L T B X V D D J M P R V P X D C E
Y R E T S Y M E U H L V J X N I H P L B I T L G
L D O A H A D G J X I A P O S S E S S I O N U O
L Z X N H L K R K G Z K I P A R A N O R M A L W
F Q Z F H Q T H L O V C G N Y G W S K A R V Z S
L U Q W M Z R P E F K U Z G G G L H T A E T L Z
```

CREEPYPASTA   ASYLUM   PENITENTIARY   EXORCISM   POSSESSION

WITCHES   SATANIC PANIC   PARANORMAL   MYSTERY   HAUNTED   SPIRITS

HORROR   DEVIL   DEMONS   GHOSTS

WHAT HAVE YOU LEARNED?

1. What type of 'panic' gripped suburban America throughout the 1980s?

_____

2. The case referenced by this phrase on a historical marker in West Virginia:
"Only known case in which testimony from a ghost helped convict a murderer."

_____

3. Famous, formidable maximum security prison that is now said to be haunted.

_____

4. What was notable about Arne Cheyenne Johnson's case?

_____

5. Name for the hearings about alleged witchcraft in the 1690s.

_____

6. Who possessed their friend and solved their own murder?

_____

7. Name for the Maria Marten case, after where her body was found.

_____

8. What's the name of a type of scary internet story, like that of Slenderman?

_____

9. What did Sarah Good say God would give her persecutors to drink?

_____

10. Brand of rifle California's Mystery House is named for.

_____

CULTS

FATAL FOLLOWERS

Use the clues below to reveal the cult-related answers to these puzzles.

1. **TEH LLVNASIU SINUITTTE** _____

2. **EVNHE'SA GEAT AAYW AMTE** _____

3. **MAPJNAHUEESRR** _____

4. **ULCT AWSERSENA ORWENTK** _____

5. **EHT ENVSE SAESL** _____

6. **EREMT-E** _____

7. **IDLOLCOLA LRISEV** _____

8. **TEELMIIF ATALROHNIBTIIE** _____

9. **LETRNAE OIAMNTNU** _____

10. **IRNNNTTEAOLIA OKHIOTGDNH** _____

▶▶▶ DO NOT CROSS ◀◀◀ ▶▶▶ STOP ◀◀◀ ▶▶▶ DO NOT CROSS ◀◀◀ ▶▶▶ STOP ◀◀◀ ▶▶▶ DO NOT CROSS ◀◀◀

CLUES

1. Group created by Saul B. Newton who taught that the traditional nuclear family was the root of modern society's issues

2. The phrase on the patches Heaven's Gate members wore as part of their mass-suicide uniform

3. Name for the commune in Oregon set up by the Rajneeshees

4. The deprogramming organization created by Ted Patrick

5. The Biblical symbols that David Karesh believed he must open to pave the way for the Second Coming

6. Device used by Scientologists to identify spiritual problems

7. Substance Amy Carlson was ingesting as a protection against COVID-19 that turned her skin blue

8. What Synanon members were told they had to go through, as it was believed that addicts would never be free of their addictions or be able to re-enter society

9. Name given to the site of the Ant Hill Kids' commune

10. The "Organization" that is the highest membership level of the Order of the Solar Temple

FINAL MESSAGE #1

Use this key to find out what message the members of Heaven's Gate left on their website before their mass suicide.

A	B	C	D	E	F	G	H	I	J	K	L	M	N	O	P	Q	R	S	T	U	V	W	X	Y	Z
							C	D																	

H _ _ _ - _ _ _ _ I _ _ _ _ _ _ _ _ _ _ _ _ _ _
C T S H   I X Y Y   I U D R O Q   N S X Q E U H   G X

H _ _ _ _ _ _ ' _ _ _ _ ... _ _ _ 22 _ _ _ _ _ _ _ _
C H T Z H R Q   O T G H   X E U   P H T U Q   X L

_ _ _ _ _ _ _ _ H _ _ _ _ _ _ _ _ _ _ _ _ _ _ H
N S T Q Q U X X   C H U H   X R   Y S T R H G   H T U G C

I _ I _ _ _ _ _ _ _ _ _ _ I _ _ _ _ _ _ _ _ _ _ _ I _ _ _
D Q   L D R T S S P   N X A D R O   G X   N X R N S E Q D X R

_ ' _ _ _ _ _ _ _ _ I _ ' _ _ _ _ H _ H _ _ _ _
O U T M E T G D X R   L U X A   G C H   C E A T R

_ _ _ _ _ _ I _ _ _ _ _ _ _ _ . _ _ _ _ _
H Z X S E G D X R T U P   S H Z H S   B H   T U H

H _ _ _ I _ _ _ _ _ _ _ _ _ _ _ _ _ H I _ _ _
C T Y Y D S P   Y U H Y T U H M   G X   S H T Z H   G C D Q

_ _ _ _ _ _ _ _ _ I _ H _ I ' _ _ _ _ .
B X U S M   T R M   G X   B D G C   G D Q   N U H B

- Heaven's Gate goodbye message -

FINAL MESSAGE #2

>>> DO NOT CROSS <<< >>> STOP <<< >>> DO NOT CROSS <<< >>> STOP <<< >>> DO NOT CROSS <<<

A	B	C	D	E	F	G	H	I	J	K	L	M	N	O	P	Q	R	S	T	U	V	W	X	Y	Z
																						X			

```
____  ___  ____  ____  __.  W_  ____
V P Y Z   C Q N   E U T Z   T N C W   Q R   X Z   E P U O

__  W_._W_  __  ___  _____.  W__  ____'
U V   O C X F   X Z   L C V   V U N Z O   X Z   O U O F V

_____  ____._W_  __  _____  __
H C W W U V   R Q U H U O Z   X Z   H C W W U V V Z O   P F

___  __  _____  _____
P H V   C T   N Z M C E Q V U C F P S   R Q U H U O Z

_____  ___  _____  __  __
B N C V Z R V U F L   V G Z   H C F O U V U C F R   C T   P F

_____  W____.
U F G Q W P F Z   X C N E O
```

- Jim Jones -

FOLLOW THE LEADER #1

DOWN

1. Branch Davidian leader David Koresh's real name
3. Original name for The Children of God cult
5. Outlawed practice that was the main reason for the FLDS split from the main church
6. Canadian cult named by its leader for the way they resembled busy worker ants while constructing the group's doomsday compound
7. The brand of drink consumed by Peoples Temple members during the mass suicide
9. A UFO following this comet was supposed to collect the souls of Heaven's Gate members from Earth after their suicides

ACROSS

2. Brand of sneakers worn by Heaven's Gate members as part of their mass-suicide uniform
4. Highest rank achieved by Scientologists, whose members sign a billion-year contract
8. Officially known as The Peoples Temple Agricultural Project, the nickname for the site of The Peoples Temple mass suicide in 1978
10. Name for the infamous standoff between ATF and the Branch Davidians
11. Cult that branded its members with the leader's initials
12. Nicknames of Bonnie Nettles and Marshall Applewhite, leaders of Heaven's Gate

>>> DO NOT CROSS <<< >>> STOP <<< >>> DO NOT CROSS <<< >>> STOP <<< >>> DO NOT CROSS <<<

FOLLOW THE LEADER #2

DOWN

1. Group that carried out the Tokyo subway sarin attacks in 1995
3. Scientology's name for the self or the soul, that is believed to have lived many past lives on alien planets
4. Cult that called themselves a "capitalistic commune", and claimed they would make members "healthy, wealthy, and wise"
6. Name for a highly confrontational approach to treatment that members of Synanon called "The Game"
7. Smallville star who famously became a higher-up in NXIVM
8. Troubling FLDS belief that claims certain sins can only be forgiven through the death of the sinner
10. Group that carried out the first bioterrorist attack in U.S. history
13. Cult led by a woman followers called "Mother God", who they believed to be 19 billion years old

ACROSS

2. Cult leader who performed a crude and brutal surgery on follower Solange Boilard, who later died of the injuries she received
5. Set of pseudoscientific ideas and practices written by L. Ron Hubbard
9. The name of the sexual indoctrination practice used by female members of The Children of God
11. Cult that began as drug treatment program Tender Loving Care
12. Cult whose members murdered a three-month old baby after their leader told them he was the antichrist
14. Song Charles Manson said held encoded details of an upcoming apocalyptic race war
15. Australian cult led by Anne Hamilton-Byrne who was attempting to create a "master race" that would survive the impending apocalypse

CULT TO LEADER/FOUNDER

Match the cult to its leader/founder.

1. The Peoples Temple

2. Branch Davidians

3. Heaven's Gate

4. Children of God

5. Order of the Solar Temple

6. The Ant Hill Kids

7. Scientology

8. The Circle of Friends

9. FLDS

10. NXIVM

11. The Manson Family

12. Love Has Won

13. Synanon

14. Rajneeshees

15. Aum Shinrikyo

16. Blackburn Cult

17. The Family

18. True Russian Orthodox Church

19. Sullivanians

20. Restoration of the 10 Commandments of God

a. Keith Raniere

b. David Koresh

c. Saul B Newton

d. Warren Jeffs

e. May Otis Blackburn

f. Mwerinde/Kibweteere

g. David Miscavige

h. Shoko Asahara

i. Bhagwan Shree Rajneesh

j. David Berg

k. Amy Carlson

l. Charles Manson

m. Nettles/Applewhite

n. Charles Dederich Sr

o. Jim Jones

p. Roch Thériault

q. George G Jurscek

r. Luc Jouret

s. Pyotr Kuznetsov

t. Anne Hamilton-Byrne

PART OF THE CULT

```
Y H L F A L B O Y R Z O Y K I R N I H S M U A E
L B R A N C H D A V I D I A N S R Y O Y Y J N L
X K D W W P K R Z Q M C E N D G B A K D A G N P
L T M O T Y Z W F C U L O V E H A S W O N H L M
P N I A H V T H E P E O P L E S T E M P L E F E
M W O Z N U C R X H S P P K G E T Q A O G Z V T
N M H N Y S N H V P I I N P N I T O J G B T Z R
W Y B P A N O V I Q V Z R E I P E Z G I T H C A
P O B A E N N N F L I K O C M R L I Q Q K E D L
Q A G L D L Y P F T D Y R C M C E Y H D C C T O
D M T P S N A S I A E R E W A X A M E U H I L S
X B T Q P U Z L J C M X E J R P D N L T U R U E
I N D O C T R I N A T I O N G X E T Z D Y C C H
H S E E H S E E N J A R L F O A R V Z G U L N T
K H O I N Y Z L A N Y Z U Y R F B N O D X E R F
L W U C H S Z B G M S N T D P N G L N C G O U O
W V W D V O W M T U Q F K C E P O O V R K F B R
Q A X E T A G S N E V A E H D T E O D G M F K E
C J E L V T N F Z W E E L Z N X H A L M L R C D
N Q H J X V E N F Y J L N E W O R A P V K I A R
E H D V Z T W Z L Y Y V I T W P G A P I X E L O
D V D H R Q B S D T Y C X F E W Y U O X A N B R
K L I N W Q W Y S V S V Y J N Z L O K N J D M J
Q C R S D I K L L I H T N A E H T E W V C S J F
```

AUM SHINRIKYO   **BLACKBURN CULT**   **RAJNEESHEES**   **SYNANON**   **LOVE HAS WON**

MANSON FAMILY   **NXIVM**   **FLDS**   **THE CIRCLE OF FRIENDS**   **SCIENTOLOGY**   **THE ANT HILL KIDS**

ORDER OF THE SOLAR TEMPLE   **CHILDREN OF GOD**   **HEAVEN'S GATE**   **BRANCH DAVIDIANS**

THE PEOPLE'S TEMPLE   **DEPROGRAMMING**   **INDOCTRINATION**   **LEADER**   **CULT**

WHAT HAVE YOU LEARNED?

1. Which cult is known for 1993's Waco siege?

_____

2. What name did Amy Carlson's followers call her?

_____

3. Which cult participated in "attack therapy"?

_____

4. What brand of shoe did all Heaven's Gate members wear for their mass suicide?

_____

5. Which comet was supposed to close Heaven's Gate?

_____

6. What act did Jim Jones say The Peoples Temple members committed?

_____

7. Why did Jim Jones say The Peoples Temple committed suicide?

_____

8. What were Bonnie Nettles and Marshall Applewhite's nicknames?

_____

9. What is flirty fishing?

_____

10. Which cult did *Smallville* actresses Kristin Kreuk and Allison Mack join?

_____

THE GOOD GUYS

DOING IT RIGHT #1

DOWN

1. Collective name for five Black and Latino teen boys falsely accused of sexually assualting a jogger in New York City in 1989
2. Author of *I'll Be Gone in the Dark*, whose investigation into the case was instrumental in identifying The Golden State Killer
3. Nonprofit organization devoted to overturning and preventing wrongful convictions
7. Man who was wrongly accused of sexual assault, who later went on to be the subject of the Neflix documentary *Making a Murderer* about a murder he may have committed

ACROSS

4. American who was the defendant in a sensational Italian trial after being accused of killing her roommate
5. Investigation tactic developed by FBI agent Robert Ressler in the 1970s
6. Collective name of three teen boys wrongly accused of the murder of three young boys in Arkansas 1993
8. Writer of *The Stranger Beside Me*, who worked with Ted Bundy at the suicide prevention hotline, and gave a tip to the police to investigate him
9. Muhammad Aziz and Khalil Islam were exonnerated in 2021 after their wrongful convictions in the assassination of this man

DOING IT RIGHT #2

DOWN

1. Subject of Bob Dylan's *Hurricane*, a boxer wrongfully accused of a 1966 murder

2. Kind of evidence used in trial that is known to be unreliable

3. Phenomenon of moral hysteria that was the reason the West Memphis Three were accused of their crimes

4. Longest wrongful imprisonment in U.S. history

6. Man whose case is one of Canada's most notorious instances of wrongful accusation

7. According to The Innocence Project, the U.S. state that has the highest incidence of wrongful conviction

ACROSS

5. Collective name for Elizabeth Ramirez, Cassandra Rivera, Kristie Mayhugh, and Anna Vasquez who were wrongfully accused of the sexual assault of minors in 1994

8. Missouri man who spent 42 years in prison for murder despite the actual killers confessing he had nothing to do with the case, and the only witness recanting her testimony

9. High-stress interrogative method developed in the 1950s that has resulted in many false confessions

JUSTICE OR? #1

Use this key to reveal what Martin Luther King Jr. and Angela Davis have said about justice and the American justice system.

A	B	C	D	E	F	G	H	I	J	K	L	M	N	O	P	Q	R	S	T	U	V	W	X	Y	Z
N									W																

```
_ _ J _ _ _ _ _   _ _ _ _ A _ _ _   _ _   _ A _   _ _ _ A _
O I W B C P O S M   N I D J A M E M   O C   N   P A E M N P

_ _   _ _ J _ _ _ _   _ _ _ _ J _ _ _ .
P Y   W B C P O S M   M X M E D J A M E M
```

- Martin Luther King Jr. -

```
J A _ _ _   _ A _   _ _ _ _ _ _   _ A _   _ _ _ _ _ _ _ _ ,
W N O V C   N I K   H E O C Y I C   N E M   K M C O L I M K

_ _   _ _ _ A _   _ _ A _   _ _ _ _ _ _ ,   _ _
P Y   U E M N R   A B T N I   U M O I L C   P Y

_ _ _ _ _ _   _ _ _   _ _ _ A _ _ _ _   _ _ _ _
S Y I X M E P   P A M   H Y H B V N P O Y I   O I P Y

_ _ _ _ _ _ _   _ _   A   _ _ _   -   _ _ _ _ _ _ _   _ _
C H M S O T M I C   O I   N   G Y Y   Y U M K O M I P   P Y

_ _ _   _ _ _ _ _ _   _ _ _   _ A _ _ _ _ _ _ _   _ _
Y B E   R M M H M E C   U B P   K N I L M E Y B C   P Y

_ A _ _   _ _ _ _ _ .
M N S A   Y P A M E
```

- Angela Davis -

JUSTICE OR? #2

Solve this puzzle to find out what social justice activist **Bryan** Stevenson had to say about the American justice system.

A	B	C	D	E	F	G	H	I	J	K	L	M	N	O	P	Q	R	S	T	U	V	W	X	Y	Z
												B					R								

```
_ _ _     _ _ _ N _ _     _ _ S _ _ _ _     _ S _ S _ _ _
G Y V     Z V K T K B F Q   X Y R N K Z L     R D R N L T

_ _ _ _ _ S     _ _ _     _ S _ _ _ _     _ _     _ _ _     _ _ _
N V L F N R     D G Y     O L N N L V     K S     D G Y     F V L

_ _ _ _     _ N _     _ _ _ _ N _     _ N _ N     _ _     _ _ _     _ _ _
V K Z J     F B P     C Y K Q N D     N J F B     K S     D G Y     F V L

_ _ _ _     _ N _     _ N N _ _ _ _ N .
W G G V     F B P     K B B G Z L B N
```

- **Bryan Stevenson** -

WRONGFUL CONVICTION

Rank these people who have been falsely **impris**oned on when they were exonerated and how long they spent in prison.

A. Damien Echols

B. Amanda Knox

C. Steven Avery

D. Central Park 5

E. San Antonio 4

F. Rubin Carter

G. Kevin Strickland

H. Steven Truscott

I. Richard Phillips

J. Glenn Ford

Exoneration Date (Most recent to longest ago)	Time in Prison (Least to most)

INNOCENCE

Use the hints below to help you reveal these justice-related terms.

1. **ASGCARIMREI OF SCTUIEJ** _____

2. **WIENTESESY EYSMOTITN** _____

3. **SLEFA NSOOFSNEIC** _____

4. **IECFSNRO NSASLYAI** _____

5. **XERPET STISNWE** _____

6. **PJYURRE** _____

7. **ITONAOINCFRM SAIB** _____

8. **OELNB EASUC PURONRITCO** _____

9. **PELA ANAIGRB** _____

10. **ITECNNON NRIR'OSSEP MMALIDE** _____

>>> DO NOT CROSS <<< >>> STOP <<< >>> DO NOT CROSS <<< >>> STOP <<< >>> DO NOT CROSS <<<

HINTS!

1. Unfair or incorrect outcome of a trial

2. Often unreliable accounts by those who claimed to witness a crime

3. Sometimes the result of coercion during police questioning

4. The Innocence Project says 44% of wrongful convictions are the result of this being ineffective or incorrect

5. Experienced person brought in to give an informed opinion on a case

6. Intentionally lying under oath

7. Psychological phenomenon that would lead an investigator to look for evidence that backs up their existing theory, instead of building a theory from existing evidence

8. For example, a police officer planting evidence because they believe the person is guilty but there is not enough evidence to convict

9. Where a defendant pleads guilty to a lesser charge in exchange for a more lenient sentence

10. The problem that arises when an innocent person could be given a reduced sentence or even be freed if they admit to the crime they did not commit

FALSE ACCUSATIONS

```
U  Y  I  M  V  O  A  V  E  M  E  C  I  J  K  F  Y  T  H  R  K  A  G  P
H  B  X  Y  R  F  X  D  Q  C  Y  A  G  P  A  S  N  W  G  B  N  V  Y  N
B  O  L  U  J  V  F  N  N  E  V  N  K  L  C  Q  O  T  Y  A  W  T  W  M
I  Z  J  Q  C  M  U  E  Z  K  I  S  S  S  C  K  M  C  F  M  P  L  S  D
L  J  F  X  Y  L  D  L  B  L  L  E  J  S  D  Q  I  V  D  F  H  I  T  Z
H  B  R  Y  V  I  L  D  I  T  C  H  E  O  G  D  T  U  F  F  L  E  L  F
G  T  Y  E  V  K  O  F  V  O  L  N  W  L  S  O  S  C  O  A  C  H  G  S
A  Z  N  E  N  V  O  M  N  J  T  U  M  W  J  O  E  I  N  O  Z  I  T  J
I  J  N  X  T  R  B  F  B  E  R  V  W  N  U  C  T  R  E  N  H  F  Q  O
Q  M  Q  F  P  Q  E  S  N  X  E  O  E  U  H  B  U  R  C  O  W  H  P  Z
E  A  F  R  U  S  X  C  S  C  C  S  Y  X  V  O  C  O  A  I  S  K  T  C
S  I  X  P  S  A  I  H  I  C  V  G  R  U  J  I  N  P  K  T  E  F  E  B
C  Y  A  I  T  N  C  T  K  L  I  Z  P  N  O  V  C  F  J  I  A  T  I  I
F  O  O  G  G  W  S  C  Q  Q  K  S  O  N  I  U  U  S  U  T  G  W  P  A
E  N  Z  O  E  U  M  R  U  B  B  I  N  C  R  M  H  P  I  E  U  X  D  S
I  W  H  N  J  K  T  H  G  S  T  X  T  E  L  E  D  L  A  P  H  L  I  Y
H  G  B  D  N  J  E  O  G  A  A  I  P  L  R  T  B  Z  Q  G  K  E  N  U
L  O  M  Y  B  S  C  R  R  I  O  T  H  L  C  O  K  Q  T  J  J  Y  N  D
U  D  E  F  E  N  S  E  V  N  J  W  I  R  T  A  F  F  C  N  A  N  O  B
T  V  Z  T  J  Q  N  Q  M  Z  W  R  D  O  N  V  F  N  S  L  J  X  C  R
A  S  D  J  D  O  V  B  M  G  Z  Z  Q  Q  N  S  K  B  W  D  W  Q  E  T
Y  M  E  S  X  B  J  W  H  J  H  R  E  N  R  Y  X  P  M  S  J  E  N  K
V  F  Q  E  Y  A  N  O  I  T  A  G  I  T  S  E  V  N  I  E  T  Q  C  R
D  J  D  I  S  C  R  I  M  I  N  A  T  I  O  N  V  T  E  C  A  R  E  D
```

FORENSICS   COERCION   FALSE CONFESSION   BIAS   DISCRIMINATION   PROFILING

JOURNALISM   INVESTIGATION   PETITION   EVIDENCE   SENTENCING   INNOCENCE   DEFENSE

JUSTICE   TESTIMONY   CONVICTION   ACCUSATION   EXONERATION

WHAT HAVE YOU LEARNED?

1. What is one of the least reliable forms of evidence?

_____

2. Which killer and personal friend did writer Ann Rule send a tip to the police about?

_____

3. What did Angela Davis compare jails and prisons to?

_____

4. Who compared the fanatic interest in the OJ SImpson trial to a soap opera obsession?

_____

5. Who was instrumental in developing criminal psychological profiling?

_____

6. Illinois is the state with the highest rate of what miscarriage of justice?

_____

7. What percentage of wrongful convictions are due to incorrect forensic analysis?

_____

8. What kind of "corruption" may result in authorities planting evidence?

_____

9. How many years did Kevin Strickland spend wrongfully imprisoned?

_____

10. What New York site was the center of a sensational 1989 case of wrongful conviction?

_____

ORGANIZED CRIME

MAFIA

Use the hints below to reveal these Mafia-related terms.

1. **EHT VEFI MLFISIEA** _____

2. **ST. EVNLE'TANIS ADY RASESCMA** _____

3. **PONIRTOCTE KTNERGRAEECI** _____

4. **HET RAPPED DNO** _____

5. **AEMAELSESCTRLMA RAW** _____

6. **CPAO AIMFAGLI** _____

7. **BYTMEIUSU** _____

8. **EHT MRIG REPAER** _____

9. **IWTENSS PRTNOCOEIT PRAORMG** _____

10. **TEH CAORONPITOR** _____

>>> DO NOT CROSS <<<   >>> STOP <<< >>> DO NOT CROSS <<< >>> STOP <<< >>> DO NOT CROSS <<<

HINTS!

1. Collective name for the Bonanno, Colombo, Gambino, Genovese, and Lucchese organizations

2. Murder of seven people associated with Chicago's North Side Gang carried out on Al Capone's orders

3. The practice of paying the Mafia to keep you safe from other criminals

4. John Gotti's nickname

5. The violent struggle for power between Joe Masseria's faction and Salvatore Maranzano's factions of the Mafia in 1930s New York

6. Italian name for the boss of a local crime family

7. Yakuza punishment where part of a person's pinky would be cut off so they could no longer properly wield a katana

8. Program created in the U.S. in the 1970s to relocate witnesses in danger of retaliation by criminals

9. Nickname for Gregory Scarpa Sr. hitman for the Colombo Family

10. Name for the Cuban Mafia founded by former police officer Jose Miguel Battle Sr.

CRIME FAMILIES #1

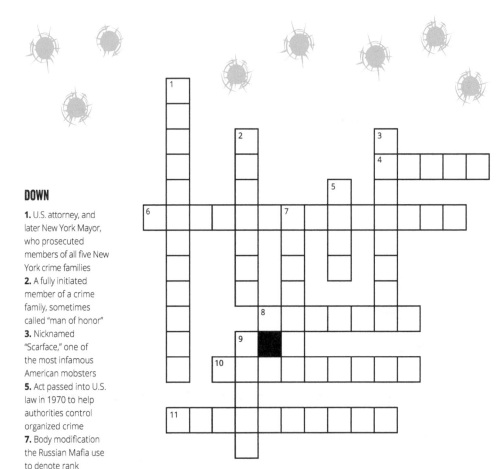

DOWN

1. U.S. attorney, and later New York Mayor, who prosecuted members of all five New York crime families
2. A fully initiated member of a crime family, sometimes called "man of honor"
3. Nicknamed "Scarface," one of the most infamous American mobsters
5. Act passed into U.S. law in 1970 to help authorities control organized crime
7. Body modification the Russian Mafia use to denote rank
9. Nickname of Benjamin Siegel

ACROSS

4. Nickname of Charles Luciano of the Genovese crime family
6. Genovese boss who would walk the streets in his bathrobe, talk to himself, and make public scenes to attempt to establish a basis for insanity were he ever arrested
8. Level of mafia membership who does the grunt work
10. Italian leader bent on taking down the mafia, leading many mobsters to move their operations to America
11. Musician Al Capone kidnapped to play at his birthday party

CRIME FAMILIES #2

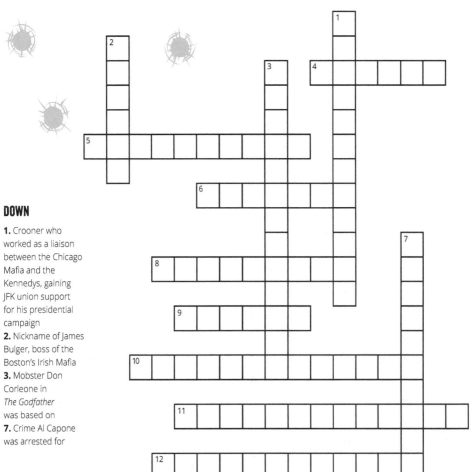

DOWN

1. Crooner who worked as a liaison between the Chicago Mafia and the Kennedys, gaining JFK union support for his presidential campaign
2. Nickname of James Bulger, boss of the Boston's Irish Mafia
3. Mobster Don Corleone in *The Godfather* was based on
7. Crime Al Capone was arrested for

ACROSS

4. Name for the Japanese Mafia
5. City where Chief of Police David Hennessy was murdered by the Mafia, inciting an angry mob to kill 11
6. Genovese boss Vincent Gigante's nickname
8. Position in a crime family known as "Capo di tutti capi"
9. Italian region where the term Mafia originated
10. TV presenter who overhyped the opening of Al Capone's vault, leading to massive disappointment when the vault only contained dirt and empty bottles
11. Name for organization set up in 1931 as the governing body of all organized crime in America
12. John Gotti's nickname

GANGSTERS #1

```
R X T O M W Q K F H T B K N K M J C X K R B G W
Q O Y I T F I N C K G G Y U W Q A J K R Y T Q C
J H Y R W A E F M O R B K U V R O V E H O L H V
P Y L I W M Z O H V H X A C L E E G P M Y A H N
J O S E P H P R O F A C I O B B L F M N R Q S C
R F N R U P I D L V E P G O E U R Y Y L C A Q Z
O Z Y D B D M W K B C A N P B N G N E A T P J F
R N Y R F Y M M F F M A F Y B A O S X J G E G D
X T A W H W T B A B N A E C G T L P A N J F I S
V X M Z A N V O I N I T J L F U L L A O V Y T P
R I C Z N N P N O C I G I B C K C V S C K V T E
X B T D F A O H E H I A E I N G B E I A L H O R
P U T O M R R N W S N T A Z M N P X E E H A G L
L G G Y G X A A I O E N H P G H C L Y V H B N J
Z S C E W E A N M X O H A Y C Z C C X H B R H Y
N Y A I W Q N I K E S Z C O P K F P D B E W O K
Q S V X A C U O D C R L L C Y Y I A Q M R O J Z
J I B Y G H V J V H O O C G U N P V T S L O W A
J E N B G Z Q S Y E M S T D R L O U H K U Q T N
V G L Y O L I P T B S X T A S R Y S J P W E T I
U E I B Y H D C O W N E I E V Y V M S E A K K Y
I L V S D H S H A W U X H J L L O H M D G X H O
K O E B I J P Z O R V X G J Q L A V I O P B V S
V I N C E N T M A N G A N O U L O S H H T I L P
```

TOMMY LUCCHESE   **VITO GENOVESE**   **CARLO GAMBINO**   **JOSEPH COLOMBO**   **JOE BONANNO**

VINCENT MANGANO   **SALVATORE MARANZANO**   **JOSEPH PROFACI**   **TOMMY GAGLIANO**

CHARLES LUCIANO   **JOHN GOTTI**   **BUGSY SIEGEL**   **FRANK COSTELLO**   **WHITEY BULGER**   **AL CAPONE**

GANGSTERS #2

```
X E O M L O R X Z P Y C T P D Z E Z Q K A C O N
W H T M O N B R E A R R Z N E T H N Q K P G Z H
X H E A J H E A I D I O O U H G D Z S Z X G Q X
U W O C I R L F R Y T I H E Y J Q M E G R G T L
H A G M W C A B M U T J G I Q O O Q B L A C L S
F D Z N M M O A S C Q O P O B B C Y S Q C D Z Q
K F Y G N R Z S E S D C E O O I Z I F P K C F Z
Q S U S B U U T S F W K O H S I T Y R Z E I I U
Q G U F K J O Z A A C E W P E M B I M O T S V T
F S Q A D R N T G R O A J C X R P G O U E N E I
N X Y L P L H Q I P E U J Q V B F L Q N E W F M
G G M E N E Y M N N A L A U W G M W A D R N A N
T O P B R B E Q F U B U W A D N X G H X I S M F
B H T K O E W O N T S B W E K I M N T K N T I W
U T I X F S R M K R D C B F U G C I Z S G K L I
K K Q O X C S A M A D E M A N G W L I M A E I X
G U D H E Q Y G K G S R W V C E O G T N V L E X
U J C R W N Y R Z M D U H E H L Y G T E J V S T
W P A B I X E U O U S N I U P T B U D U S A Y I
L B P Q F I E I S B W Y U D I O P M U N K T S C
S R O Z D G I U U D S X R N Q O V S E G G P I B
A A F L J C W K Z L E X Y L X B F H R C P E P Z
E N O H M B N T I T H E C O M M I S S I O N U R
X S V O T I U X X T F A P K C T U G O T K W J Y
```

ENFORCER   BOSS   CAPO   SOLDIER   THE COMMISSION   THE GODFATHER   ASSOCIATE

RICO   PROTECTION   RACKETEERING   BOOTLEGGING   SMUGGLING   PROHIBITION   MADE MAN

G-MEN   FIVE FAMILIES   CRIME   YAKUZA   MOB   MAFIA

MOBSTER MINDSET #1

Use this key to reveal what two famous Mafia figures had to say about the hypocrisy of American society.

A	B	C	D	E	F	G	H	I	J	K	L	M	N	O	P	Q	R	S	T	U	V	W	X	Y	Z
		H												J											

_ _ _ _ _ _ ,   _ _ _ _ _ _ _ ,   _ _ _   _ _ O _ _ _   _ C _ _ _ _
O Z B A R C   K S T V R G C   S W B   Y J K F P H F S W C

_ _ _ _   _   _ _ C _ _ _ _   _ O   _ _ _ _ _ .   _ _   _ O _ '
N S D R   S   K F H R W C R   P J   C P R S K   T R   B J W P

_ _ _ _   O _ _ .
W R R B   J W R

- Carlo Gambino -

C _ _ _ _ _ _ _ _   _ _   _ _ _   _ _ _ _ _ _ _ _
H S Y F P S K F C U   F C   P N R   K R A F P F U S P R

_ _ C _ _ _   O _   _ _ _   _ _ _ _ _ _   C _ _ _ _ .
G S H E R P   J I   P N R   G Z K F W A   H K S C C

- Al Capone -

MOBSTER MINDSET #2

Use this key to reveal some advice from two famous Mafia members.

A	B	C	D	E	F	G	H	I	J	K	L	M	N	O	P	Q	R	S	T	U	V	W	X	Y	Z
						X						V													

```
                            L
__  ___  ____  _  ___  __  ____
Z S  A P H  O G B L  G  V P M  P S  Y O G M

          L                        G
_____  ____  ___  ____ '  ___ ,  ____
Q L P Q V L  Y G D M  G D C  I G D M  X L M  M O L D

              L                    ,
___  ___  _____  ___  _____  ___
A P H  I G D  T H Q Q V A  M O L  C L R G D C  G D C

        L        G .
_____  __  ___  ____
T O P B L V  Z D  M O L  C P H X O
```

- Lucky Luciano -

```
            G
___  ___  ___  ____  _____  ____  _
A P H  I G D  X L M  R H I O  S H F M O L F  Y Z M O  G

                    G
____  ____  ___  _  ___  ____  ___
N Z D C  Y P F C  G D C  G  X H D  M O G D  A P H

            L    .
___  ____  _  ____  ____  _____
I G D  Y Z M O  G  N Z D C  Y P F C  G V P D L
```

- Al Capone -

WHAT HAVE YOU LEARNED?

1. Which Genovese boss was known as "The Chin"?

_____

2. "Lucky" was the nickname of which Genovese boss?

_____

3. Al Capone said you can get far with a **kind word** and what object?

_____

4. Who did Carlo Gambino say had a license to steal?

_____

5. Yubitsume is a punishment practised **by which** group?

_____

6. What year was RICO enacted in the U.S.?

_____

7. Frank Costello was the inspiration for **which fictional** character?

_____

8. How many New York crime families **are there**?

_____

9. What is the name for people who work **with** the Mafia but are not actually in the family?

_____

10. What did Al Capone call a "legitimate **racket**"?

_____

UNSOLVED MYSTERIES

MYSTIFYING CASES #1

DOWN

1. Name for the killer who murdered at least five women in Whitechapel, London, in 1888

2. Brand of painkiller tampered with in Chicago in 1982, leading to the deaths of seven people

3. Six-year-old beauty queen who was murdered in Boulder, Colorado in 1996

4. Country where Kris Kremers and Lisanne Froon went missing while hiking, leaving behind mysterious photos on their camera

5. Floral nickname of Elizabeth Short

7. Phrase on the slip of paper found in the Somerton Man's pocket*

9. Weapon used in the Hinterkaifek murders, the Villisca murders, and a series of slayings in New Orleans, all unsolved

ACROSS

6. Unknown murderer who terrorized northern California in the late 1960s

8. The murder of this family in the Setagaya neighbourhood of Tokyo in 2000 remains unsolved, despite the perpetrator leaving behind 10 personal items

This case was solved during publication!

MYSTIFYING CASES #2

DOWN

1. Dessert shop in Austin that was the site of a brutal, unsolved quadruple homicide

3. Young Canadian woman found dead in the water tank on the roof of the Cecil Hotel

5. Man who successfully hijacked a plane in 1971 and disappeared with $200,000 in ransom money

6. Town on the Texas/Arkansas border that was the site of a series of lovers' lane attacks

ACROSS

2. Town in Ohio terrorized by an unknown letter writer who seemed to be exposing town secrets

4. Last name of three children who disappeared from a South Australian beach on Australia Day 1966

7. Ship whose crew vanished, leaving behind six months of supplies and all personal belongings

8. Last name of the five children who disappeared during a house fire on Christmas Eve 1945

9. Nickname for balaclava-clad home invader who abused three children in Melbourne, Australia

10. Name for the site of the mysterious deaths of nine hikers in 1959

11. Name for the murders of Abigail Williams and Liberty German; the subject of the podcast *Down the Hill*

CASE NOT CLOSED

Use the hints below to help you unscramble these mysterious terms.

1. **HWO TPU LAEBL NI HTE HCWY MEL** _____

2. **DWON EHT LIHL** _____

3. **HTE NTWO HATT REDDDAE NUDWONS** _____

4. **SI SNIIFDHE** _____

5. **SLMLA OENGRIF ANTIOCF** _____

6. **HGIET ADY BEDRI** _____

7. **RAOONTAC** _____

8. **MLYAIASA NRILASIE** _____

9. **HVNEGIRYTE SI ESGELINMSAN** _____

10. **OSSNONETPUA AHNMU UCTBOMSNIO** _____

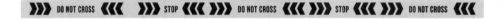

⟩⟩⟩ **DO NOT CROSS** ⟨⟨⟨   ⟩⟩⟩ **STOP** ⟨⟨⟨ ⟩⟩⟩ **DO NOT CROSS** ⟨⟨⟨ ⟩⟩⟩ **STOP** ⟨⟨⟨ ⟩⟩⟩ **DO NOT CROSS** ⟨⟨⟨

HINTS!

1. Graffiti found on a wall in Birmingham, relating to an unidentified woman's body that was found in a tree in Hagley Wood in 1943

2. The words heard on a Snapchat video found on the phone of one of the victims in the Delphi Murders case

3. The 1976 movie inspired by the Texarkana lovers' lane murders

4. What the phrase "tamam shud" roughly translates to (See bottom of page 96)

5. What the alleged kidnappers said they represented in the JonBenet Ramsey ransom note

6. Name for the case of the strange death of Christina Kettlewell who apparently drowned in nine inches of water, 150 feet away from the cottage she was staying at, which mysteriously burned down the same night

7. Word carved into a palisade fence at the site of the missing colony of Roanoke

8. The airline that missing Flight 370 belonged to

9. Last words of Ecclesiastes 12:8, connected to the bizarre death of Charles Morgan in 1977

10. Name for the heavily debated idea that a person can simply burst into flames, that some think was the cause of Mary Reeser's death

STILL SEARCHING

```
M U M E G N A R T S D D S U D B R F T U P D S Q
J P K Y L Q V V O T M S W C L H Z X K C F C P G
O V T V S C A U N S O L V E D T I R G C V D Y X
R H T I A T F A S Q H T F H E F X Y T I N G R B
X B K Y N D E N R N X Z Z R K C X M U W U N E X
Y Q K V O A L R V H W T C W O O P K V D F K H A
H D I A N R I G Y J Z E Z G Y E H Q O A C E G G
P H Y E Y N J P S D S N N D U I F H T Y I A Z G
C O W I M X F U X W M Q E C N E D I V E M V N D
A D E A O M C K N G M S X R P Y A B D E K I D E
M Z Z B U G C I T E U J E X O T T Y O H S N V M
R B B K S K Q L N A X E B F R W C D Z S X Z M F
U U I R U G A G U V P P V C J C H V I W M K Q W
A M L I O G P A I E E H L N R X T M B J P A S J
M N D O W M P B J E S S W A F Y S U J V H I A F
W A J M C X U B H S E O T A I U H V T S H Z I T
S Y Y R B M B T S S N U M I S N X U U D L E V A
S V N Q T I D H A K H T I M G E E F Z R C I A W
M H G M Z C F C N D V X C G Z A I D Z E G W C K
M L M A X H D U I I F D B Q Q N T R O C J S J E
S D R S C L U W W S X I K I Z C V I O U R G D G
O R U A O Y E A P B I C J S Y S T H O E F S O I
E L W C J Z O X Q E G G K B A E Z D G N H P H U
G H W H H A R A E P P A S I D L C X N Q V T E R
```

**COLD CASE   THEORIES   CLUES   EVIDENCE   INVESTIGATION
STRANGE   MYSTERY   MISSING   SECRET   DISAPPEAR   BIZARRE
ANONYMOUS   UNEXPLAINED   UNKNOWN   UNSOLVED**

MESSAGES TO VICTIMS #1

A good mystery always comes along with **some** sort of spooky correspondence. Solve these puzzles to reveal what some killers, stalkers, hijackers, and watchers had to say to their victims.

A	B	C	D	E	F	G	H	I	J	K	L	M	N	O	P	Q	R	S	T	U	V	W	X	Y	Z
											T														

```
_  L___    _LL___    _____    __  __  __
U  TUNA    NUTTUPY   QAERDZA    UI  UZ  ZS

____  ___.  __  __  ____  ___  ____
ODEJ  KDP   UI  UZ  OSWA  KDP  IJRP

_LL___    __L_   ____   __   ___   _____
NUTTUPY   VUTM   YROA   UP   IJA   KSWAZI

_____    ___   __   ___   ____
QAERDZA    ORP   UZ   IJA   OSZI

_____   _____   L__   _LL   __   __LL.
MRPYAWSDZ   RPUORT   SK    RTT   IS   NUTT
```

- First line of the Zodiac Killer Cipher -

MESSAGES TO VICTIMS #2

A	B	C	D	E	F	G	H	I	J	K	L	M	N	O	P	Q	R	S	T	U	V	W	X	Y	Z
			T												K										

```
                            D        D                        D
__   ____   ___   _____   _____   _____
D    X R L Y   Y X Q   C P L T A G T   Y C Q P H R L T


D                     5 P
_____   __   ____   __   ____ ,
T Q M M R A H   V J   K E   D L   O R H C


                         $ 2 0            ,   P
_____   __           _____ ,  ___   __
G F O M P H D U G M J   D L           V D M M H   K P Y   D L


       P
_   _____ .   _____   ____   ____
R   S L R K H R O S   D   X R L Y   Y X Q   V R O S


P                           D
_____   ___   ___   _____
K R A R O C P Y G H   R L T   Y X Q   Z A Q L Y


P                               D,
_____   ____   __   ____   _   _____
K R A R O C P Y G H   X C G L   X G   M R L T   D   X R L Y


                         D                        .
_   ____   _____   _____   __   _____   __
R   Z P G M   Y A P O S   A G R T J   Y Q   A G Z P G M   L Q


                    '        D              .
_____   _____   __   ___   __   ___   ___
Z P L L J   H Y P Z Z   Q A   D M M   T Q   Y C G   B Q V
```

- D. B. Cooper -

MESSAGES TO VICTIMS #3

A	B	C	D	E	F	G	H	I	J	K	L	M	N	O	P	Q	R	S	T	U	V	W	X	Y	Z
	D												G												

```
_ O    _ O    _ _    _ _ _    _ O _ _ _ _    _ .    _ _ _ _
A G    O T G W    L A    W C I    Z G Y Z V U Y    L    T C H V

_ _ _ _ _ _    _ O _    _ _ _    _ O _ _ _    _ O
O C L A V S    N G U    A T V    F G R L Z V    A G

_ _ _ _ _ _    _ _    _ O _    _ _ _    _ B _ _    _ _ _ _ _ _
Z C F A M U V    W V    N G U    A T V    D R C Z X    S C T R L C

_ _ _ _ _ _ ,    _ B _    _ _ _ _    _ O _ .    _ _    _ O _ O
X L R R L Y K    D M A    T C H V    Y G A    L    C W    A G G

_ _ _ _ O    _ _    _    _ O _ _ _    _ O    _ _ _ _    _ _ _ _ _ _
W M Z T    G N    C    Z G O C U S    A G    A M U Y    W I E V R N

_ _ ,    _ O    _ _ _ _ _    _ _    _ _ _    _ B _ _    _ _ _    _ O _ _
L Y    E G    A T L E    L E    A T V    D V E A    O C I    G M A

_ O _    _ _    _ .    _ O _ _ _ _ _    _ _ _ ' _    _ _ _ _ _ _
N G U    W V    L    Z G M R S Y A    T V R F    W I E V R N

_ O _    _ _ _ _ ,    _ O    _ _ _ _ .    _ O _ _ _ ,    _ _ _ _ .
N G U    A T C A    G U    A T L E    E G U U I    W C U I
```

- Alleged Black Dahlia confession letter, Anonymous -

MESSAGES TO VICTIMS #4

A	B	C	D	E	F	G	H	I	J	K	L	M	N	O	P	Q	R	S	T	U	V	W	X	Y	Z
								X																	

```
_ _ _    _ I _ _ I _ _ I :    _ _ _ _    _ _ _ _    _ _ _ _
F L T    B X E E X T O X A    T P K M    K J K M    Q L N F

_ _ _ _ I _ :    _ _ ' _    _ _ I    _ _ _ _    _ _ _ _ _ _ I
F K T T X A    Y N G P    E X A    J R A G    C W A T P X N G A Y

_ _ _ _    _ _ _ I _ _    _ I . I    _ _ _ _    _ _ _ _
K V N W P    F A A P X G B    R X F    X    H G N J    J R A L A

_ _ _    _ I _ :    I' _ _    _ _ _ _    _ _ _ _ I _ _
M N W    E X I A    X I A    V A A G    N V T A L I X G B

_ _ _ _    _ _ _ _ _    _ _ _    _ _ _ _    _ _ _    _ _ I _
M N W L    R N W T A    K G Y    H G N J    M N W    R K I A

_ _ I _ _ _ _ _ .    _ _ I _    I _    _ _ _ _    _ _ _ _ _
U R X E Y L A G    P R X T    X T    G N    S N H A    O E A K T A

_ _ _ _    I _    _ _ _ I _ _ _    _ I _ _ _ _ _ .
P K H A    X P    T A L X N W T    A I A L M N G A

_ _ _ _ _ _ _ _    _ _ _    _ _ _ _    _ _ _ I _ _ I _ . _ I _
U N G U A L G A Y    R K T    V A A G    G N P X Q X A Y    X P

_ I _ _    _ _    _ _ _ _    _ _ _ _ .
J X E E    V A    N I A L    T N N G
```

- Circleville Letter Writer -

MESSAGES TO VICTIMS #5

A	B	C	D	E	F	G	H	I	J	K	L	M	N	O	P	Q	R	S	T	U	V	W	X	Y	Z
	U				C																				

```
              F
___ ___ ___   ___ ___   ___ ___ ___   ___ ___ ___ ___ ___ ___ ___   ___ ___ ___   ___ ___ ___ ___ ___   ___ ___
 B   T   T     W   C     E   X   Y     M   H   O   G   W   M   J     B   O   G     G   W   W   K   J     H   O


          B
6  5  7   ___ ___ ___ ___ ___ ___ ___ ___ ___   ___ ___ ___ ___ ___   ___ ___   ___ ___   ___ ___ ___ ___ ___
           U   W   Q   T   Y   L   B   K   G     B   T   T   W   M     F   Y     E   W     M   B   E   V   X


___ ___ ___   ___ ___ ___   ___ ___ ___ ___ ___   ___ ___ ___   ___ ___   ___ ___ ___   ___ ___ ___ ___
 I   W   Q     B   O   G     E   K   B   V   P     I   W   Q     B   J     I   W   Q     F   W   L   Y


                                        .                            ?
___ ___ ___ ___ ___ ___ ___   ___ ___ ___   ___ ___ ___ ___ ___   ___ ___ ___   ___ ___   ___   ___   ___ ___
 E   X   K   W   Q   Z   X     E   X   Y     X   W   Q   J   Y     M   X   W     B   F     H     H     B   F


                                                            B
___ ___ ___   ___ ___ ___ ___ ___ ___ ___   ___ ___ ___   ___ ___ ___ ___   ___ ___ ___ ___   ___ ___
 E   X   Y     M   B   E   V   X   Y   K     B   O   G     X   B   L   Y     U   Y   Y   O     H   O


                      F   6  5  7   B                                         F
___ ___ ___ ___ ___ ___ ___   ___ ___           ___ ___ ___ ___ ___ ___ ___ ___ ___   ___ ___ ___
 V   W   O   E   K   W   T     W   C             U   W   Q   T   Y   L   B   K   G     C   W   K


              B                               F
___ ___ ___   ___ ___ ___ ___ ___ ___   ___ ___ ___ ___   ___ ___   ___ ___ ___   ___ ___ ___ ___ ___ ___ ___
 E   X   Y     U   Y   E   E   Y   K     D   B   K   E     W   C     E   M   W     G   Y   V   B   G   Y   J


          .
___ ___ ___
 O   W   M
```

- The Watcher -

WHAT HAVE YOU LEARNED?

1. How much money did D. B. Cooper request in his note?

   _____

2. Who did the person who admitted to the Black Dahlia murder apologize to in their note?

   _____

3. What did the person who wrote the residents of 657 Boulevard call themself?

   _____

4. What town is known as The Town that Dreaded Sundown?

   _____

5. How many victims were there in the Tylenol Murders?

   _____

6. What did the Zodiac Killer say was the most dangerous animal?

   _____

7. In what kind of tree was an unidentified woman found in Hagley Wood?

   _____

8. The phrase "down the hill" relates to what murders?

   _____

9. On what day did the Beaumont children disappear?

   _____

10. JonBenet Ramsey's death and the disappearance of the Sodder children happened around what holiday?

    _____

TERRORISM AND
MASS INCIDENTS

FEAR AT LARGE

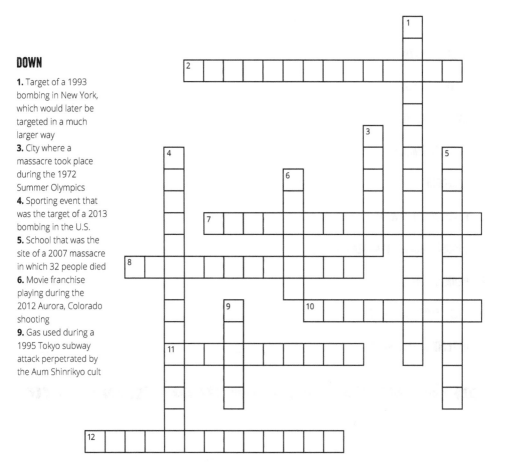

DOWN

1. Target of a 1993 bombing in New York, which would later be targeted in a much larger way

3. City where a massacre took place during the 1972 Summer Olympics

4. Sporting event that was the target of a 2013 bombing in the U.S.

5. School that was the site of a 2007 massacre in which 32 people died

6. Movie franchise playing during the 2012 Aurora, Colorado shooting

9. Gas used during a 1995 Tokyo subway attack perpetrated by the Aum Shinrikyo cult

ACROSS

2. Kind of terrorism that is backed and funded by a government

7. Man who carried out the Oklahoma City Bombings

8. State in which Flight 93 crashed on 9/11

10. Over 600 people died in these massacres in the DRC in 2008, perpetrated by the Lord's Resistance Army

11. FBI code name for the anthrax attacks in the U.S. in 2001

12. Period of the French Revolution during which François-Noël Babeuf coined the term "terrorism"

TERRORIZED PUBLIC

Use the hints below to reveal these terrorism-related words and phrases.

1. **OIIATDNIARAZCL** _____

2. **HCNFRE TOINUVLEOR** _____

3. **EMRRSORROAGTI** _____

4. **GREGNEIFRMNAO** _____

5. **YOLEGOID** _____

6. **GAIOILOBLC ARRWEAF** _____

7. **LAGBOL RMORERSTI ADBEAAST** _____

8. **REBMCERTRYISOR** _____

9. **LSEFA ALGF AOONTEIRP** _____

10. **DSTEDINIS ISMRTREOR** _____

>>> DO NOT CROSS <<< >>> STOP <<< >>> DO NOT CROSS <<< >>> STOP <<< >>> DO NOT CROSS <<<

HINTS!

1. The process of a person or group beginning to believe extremist views

2. The conflict during which the term "terrorism" was coined

3. An attack on the food supply chain or agriculture of a targeted population

4. Deliberately instilling undue panic in a population

5. A set of beliefs

6. Using viruses or bacteria in a large-scale attack

7. Catalogue of terrorist incidents from 1970 onwards

8. The use of computers to launch attacks on important systems

9. An act of terror perpetrated by a state against its own people that is then blamed on another nation or group

10. Acts of violence by non-state groups against governments or other authorities

TERRORISM

```
M N Z S F D T B A F H P X C N L O U U G S N Y O
S A E E Z Q M E W S V D K T I N W F S W V A A X
U T T Z G C E X R I P T F B Y T X S D J F L G P
Z W I Z L I Z Y H R N T J U Z F S V U K U C E S
I I L B I N J Y F I O T T M J C S E R A S Q N A
X T L P G O X G P B N R E W S X Y K M R Z H D F
N T G Z T A P J K F T S I R Z C Y Z O O A N A E
T O X C U O V E D R F G J S N C O T E T D C O B
B S I L P E D O B A S X U F M A A T P Y H B E B
K H I T U H M S E I F F P Q E R T M T K K G X S
T S S M C E O T H Q Y L X L O T Y I K T H Q B Y
N V E V E A A P W X J C L B A A R M O W H V V U
C F B I R R F F Y S R A A E N U C W U N N R U E
E C D O Z B T T Z E T L R L C T R A S Q A B D Q
I Y Z L R I U X T N L H A E G D R L J M H L L S
N S L E F B V A E O T C S G N I K C A J I H J S
U L B N A O L M C X I D P B U Q T K S M V M Y X
R M X C L I N B J T N L M O B I L I Z I N G E W
S N W E A O F M I A K U D N E T W O R K S K H I
Q P O T R I R L L Z X J R O S U O I G I L E R X
D J I I V W O E C L L F D U Y C Y N K I F N D S
S O V F L P M V A T T A C K G S U O M Y N O N A
N N J L D O X I F P C E R J N W I B Y Z Q Z G J
E D Y V H X T E R Z K B R T G E R M V P P D A N
```

RETALIATION   ENVIRONMENTAL   RELIGIOUS   ANONYMOUS   POLITICAL   COLLABORATORS

NETWORKS   MOBILIZING   EXTREMIST   HOMELAND SECURITY   DOMESTIC   INTERNATIONAL   FBI

FACTION   AGENDA   THREAT   ATTACK   VIOLENCE   HIJACKING   TERRORISM

JUSTIFIED TERROR?

Solve this puzzle to find out what Professor Martin Rudner had to say about the idea of a justified act of terrorism.

A	B	C	D	E	F	G	H	I	J	K	L	M	N	O	P	Q	R	S	T	U	V	W	X	Y	Z
											S		U												

```
_ _ _ _ _   _ _   _ _ _   _ _ _ _ _   _ _ _ _ _ _ _N :
M A L K L   G R   M A L   B H J Q C R   R M H M L J L U M

' N _   _ N'   _ _ _ _ _ _ _ _   _ _   _ _ _ _N _ _
Q U L   J H U R   M L K K Q K G R M   G R   H U Q M A L K

_ _ _N'   _ _ _ _ _ _ _   _ _ _ _ _ _',   _ _ _   _ _
J H U R   B K L L N Q J   B G F A M L K   I C M   M A H M   G R

_ _ _ _ _ L   _ _ _ _L _ _ _N ...   _ _N   _ _ _   _ _N _
F K Q R R S Z   J G R S L H N G U F   Q U L   V H U   A H D L

_   _ _ _ _ L _ _ _ _   _ _ _ _ L _ _ _   _ _ _ N _ _
H   X L K B L V M S Z   I L H C M G B C S   V H C R L   H U N

_ _ _   _ _   _ _ L   _ _ _ _ _ _   _ _ _ _ _ _ _ _
Z L M   G B   Q U L   V Q J J G M R   M L K K Q K G R M

_ _ _ _ ',   _ _   _ _   _ _ _ _ _ _ _ _   _ _ _ _ L _ _ .
H V M R   G M   G R   M L K K Q K G R J   K L F H K N S L R R
```

- Professor Martin Rudner -

WHAT HAVE YOU LEARNED?

1. What group might dissident terrorists attack?

_____

2. Contaminating livestock feed is an example of what kind of terrorism?

_____

3. Hacking could be considered what kind of terrorism?

_____

4. Hezbollah, a government-backed militant group, is an example of what kind of group?

_____

5. The Munich massacre took place during what sporting event?

_____

6. The famous phrase says "one man's terrorist is another man's" what?

_____

7. If you start to believe extremist views, you are said to have been what?

_____

8. The sarin attacks of 1995 took place in what city?

_____

9. The anthrax attacks of 2001 are an example of what kind of terrorism?

_____

10. In what year were the initial attacks on New York's World Trade Center?

_____

CRIMINOLOGY

SCIENCE OF CRIME

```
P  Q  S  X  G  Y  T  Q  P  J  S  N  K  U  E  K  N  W  Q  E  G  Q  N  V
Z  A  I  I  L  S  G  I  N  I  S  C  I  S  N  E  R  O  F  K  P  H  C  J
T  H  K  N  N  D  Q  O  A  H  E  Y  S  I  T  R  O  M  R  O  G  I  R  W
V  X  L  N  Z  D  I  W  L  V  Y  T  R  J  M  G  Q  P  Q  M  B  N  E  G
O  S  H  O  S  T  N  Y  I  O  E  T  Z  J  R  Y  X  G  Q  I  S  J  C  A
Y  E  A  C  C  T  D  Q  S  N  O  L  C  Q  Q  W  J  Y  L  O  F  D  V
D  U  T  E  R  H  E  G  T  R  H  I  E  I  H  X  W  O  O  Z  Z  E  J  W
I  B  J  N  K  N  P  I  S  N  F  K  M  J  U  V  H  N  D  F  F  E  P  B
H  B  L  T  C  X  M  A  Y  S  H  T  G  I  A  G  I  R  F  E  B  Q  Q  F
O  Z  S  E  L  O  Y  H  R  Q  T  X  T  O  R  M  W  A  N  L  A  J  F  F
C  P  X  N  N  M  G  I  H  G  B  N  Y  R  U  C  I  S  O  L  L  A  Z  G
B  M  V  Y  G  P  O  C  A  M  Y  R  I  L  I  Y  E  O  E  V  L  E  I  H
T  X  M  P  J  T  L  M  Z  Q  Z  L  Q  R  H  A  D  Y  U  H  I  L  V  F
P  J  E  O  Y  D  O  L  K  T  M  Q  O  K  P  S  L  A  O  C  S  P  I  S
J  D  Q  S  K  W  C  K  G  E  N  X  L  P  P  R  N  L  H  O  T  M  L  S
R  U  X  R  W  D  I  H  B  C  N  Z  I  A  V  I  E  Y  D  P  I  G  N  U
L  V  T  V  F  Q  X  F  Q  F  L  U  T  A  T  P  U  G  E  E  C  C  S  G
G  Q  H  B  V  N  O  D  Y  T  Y  T  A  T  A  T  T  E  N  V  S  N  O  F
N  A  O  V  C  K  T  L  J  Z  E  K  C  H  R  N  I  J  W  I  J  A  E  W
R  V  Y  B  E  J  T  Z  R  R  G  F  Q  Y  E  M  B  U  Q  G  F  Y  A  G
N  N  S  E  T  A  E  J  W  I  C  X  J  W  S  Y  C  V  Q  C  D  V  G  Y
T  F  O  T  R  H  Y  U  B  S  E  Y  W  W  X  I  E  A  E  C  Z  W  X  F
Q  W  V  C  V  S  D  N  A  P  R  O  F  I  L  E  I  S  I  U  A  Z  N  X
O  A  B  Y  F  A  U  T  O  P  S  Y  J  T  S  Y  R  D  J  T  Q  E  M  M
```

ACQUITTAL   GUILTY   INNOCENT   OBJECTION   DEFENSE   PLEA   TESTIMONY   TRIAL

RIGOR MORTIS   EVIDENCE   POLYGRAPH   FORENSICS   CRIMINOLOGY   BALLISTICS   DNA PROFILE

BLOOD SPATTER   TOXICOLOGY   AUTOPSY   FINGERPRINTS   LUMINOL

LANGUAGE OF CRIME

Use the hints below to help you unscramble these criminology and forensics-related words.

1. **LLMIOUN** _____

2. **RECSEA OBOLRSMO** _____

3. **IRPSTNNRIEFG** _____

4. **EHBNC AITLR** _____

5. **ISESNCFOR** _____

6. **OOLDB TPRTAES** _____

7. **ODCL SCEA** _____

8. **SCCAROESY** _____

9. **CHRAES WTARRNA** _____

10. **MSCLANRTTIUCAI NCEEVIDE** _____

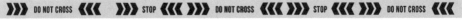

>>> DO NOT CROSS <<< >>> STOP <<< >>> DO NOT CROSS <<< >>> STOP <<< >>> DO NOT CROSS <<<

HINTS!

1. Substance used by investigators to illuminate blood traces at a crime scene

2. Known as the father of modern criminology

3. What investigators might dust for at a crime scene

4. The name for a trial that does not involve a jury, only a judge

5. The study of scientific techniques used to solve crime

6. A pattern of a bodily fluid analyzed by experts at violent crime scenes

7. An investigation that has remained unsolved and without new leads for three years

8. A person who assisted a perpetrator in a crime

9. Legal document required by law enforcement to enter and investigate certain places

10. Kind of "proof" that isn't based in science, but is inferred based on other factors

INVESTIGATION #1

Answer each of the following crime-related questions. The first letter of each answer will reveal one of the four types of serial killers, according to criminologist Ronald Holmes.

1. ☐ ☐ ☐ ☐ ☐ ☐ ☐ ☐ ☐

French term used in relation to jury selection   _____

Truman Capote novel based on the Clutter
family murders   _____

Podcast which brought the case of Adnan
Syed to public attention   _____

Serial killer who drew 11 skulls in his own blood,
thought to represent his 11 alleged victims   _____

Football player and movie star who was
the defendant in a sensational 1995 trial   _____

Last name of Scottish killer Dennis, aka
The Muswell Hill Murderer   _____

Official legal name for judging a defendant
not guilty of a crime   _____

New York mayor during the 9/11 attacks   _____

French serial killer aka The Pillow Killer
who may have killed 150 people   _____

〉〉〉 DO NOT CROSS 〈〈〈 〉〉〉 STOP 〈〈〈 〉〉〉 DO NOT CROSS 〈〈〈 〉〉〉 STOP 〈〈〈 〉〉〉 DO NOT CROSS 〈〈〈

Hint: This type of killer is motivated by hallucinations that are telling them to commit crimes. This is usually the result of psychosis and results in random victims and little or no effort to cover their tracks.

INVESTIGATION #2

2. ☐ ☐ ☐ ☐ ☐ ☐ ☐

Ship whose entire crew mysteriously
disappeared   _____

Evidence that cannot be used in a trial   _____

Nickname for killer David Berkowitz   _____

Punishment given to a defendant
found guilty of a crime   _____

Nickname of Richard Kuklinski who
claimed to be a Mafia hitman   _____

Killing partner of Henry Lee Lucas   _____

City where Delphine LaLaurie lived   _____

Hint: This killer is motivated by the belief they need to eradicate a certain group of individuals for the good of society. This results in organized, targeted attacks that are usually quick, as the killer is not getting any sadistic pleasure out of prolonging the death of their victims.

INVESTIGATION #3

3. □ □ □ □ □ □ □ □ □

Term for a jury that cannot come to a unanimous decision

_____

Combined term of The Golden State Killer's two original nicknames

_____

Ed and Lorraine Warren's area of study

_____

City where Timothy McVeigh carried out a massive bombing

_____

Cult joined by _Smallville_ actress Allison Mack

_____

Nickname of Gary Ray Bowles, after the highway where he killed

_____

Legal order to appear in court to give testimony

_____

Crime that mobster Al Capone was actually arrested for

_____

The action of looking into the cause of a crime

_____

Questioning of a witness by the opposition

_____

▶▶▶ DO NOT CROSS ◀◀◀ ▶▶▶ STOP ◀◀◀ ▶▶▶ DO NOT CROSS ◀◀◀ ▶▶▶ STOP ◀◀◀ ▶▶▶ DO NOT CROSS ◀◀◀

Hint: This type of killer kills for pleasure. Sub-categories include lust, thrill, and comfort, or profit killers.

INVESTIGATION #4

4. ☐ ☐ ☐ ☐ ☐

The name for the supervised release of a prisoner after they have served part of their sentence

_____

Word used in court when a lawyer has an issue with the presentation of evidence or a statement made by the other side

_____

Middle name of killers John Gacy and Elmer Henley

_____

Word for the proof used in court to either convict or exonerate a defendant

_____

Name for the American organized crime law put into place in 1970

_____

Hint: This type of killer is all about controlling their victims. They are usually calm, careful, and organized, and may keep trophies from their kills to remind them of the feeling of domination.

WHAT HAVE YOU LEARNED?

1. Cesare Lombroso is known as the father of what?

   _____

2. How many jurors are used on a bench trial?

   _____

3. Authorities are not allowed to enter your home to investigate without what?

   _____

4. A suspect seen running from the scene of a crime is an example of what kind of evidence?

   _____

5. What substance would an investigator use to look for blood stains?

   _____

6. If you helped someone commit a crime you may be charged as what?

   _____

7. Ballistics and fingerprint analysis are examples of what kind of science?

   _____

8. If a case has no more leads and remains unsolved it can be called what?

   _____

9. This kind of killer is motivated by a belief that they must eradicate a certain population.

   _____

10. This kind of killer is purely motivated by pleasure.

   _____

CONCLUSION

Good work, detective! You sure put your investigative skills and true crime knowledge to the test to solve these puzzles. But the fun doesn't stop there! As enjoyable as solving puzzles can be, the rewards of completing them actually reach way beyond that fleeting moment of satisfaction. You may not have realized it, but you were also honing some pretty important life skills while you searched for these solutions.

Ernő Rubik, the famous Hungarian inventor of the Rubik's Cube, said, "The problems of puzzles are very near the problems of life." He believes that all the skills required to complete a puzzle can be transferred to our real lives, and help us be better at finding appropriate solutions to our everyday issues.

Puzzles require us to look at things from many angles and try several different solutions when our initial hunch was wrong.

They force us to push through the discomfort and disappointment of failures in order to find the right answer.

They allow us to discover our capabilities and increase our confidence by presenting us with something that initially seems impossible but becomes clearer the more we focus and work through it.

Lastly, and maybe most importantly, puzzles are fun! Although the subjects of the puzzles in this book were pretty intense, the puzzles themselves were not. They are not to be taken too seriously. That's a great reminder for when life's problems get you down; most things really aren't as serious as you think they are.

So, congratulations! You haven't only found the solutions to these puzzles, you've equipped yourself with the tools to solve your real-life problems as well!

Case closed.

SOLUTIONS

HEAVY HITTERS

NOTORIOUS KILLERS CROSSWORD #1

Down: **1)** Gary Ridgway **2)** Lizzie Borden **3)** Axeman of New Orleans **4)** Zodiac Killer **5)** James French **6)** Ted Bundy **7)** Black Dahlia **9)** Richard Chase **12)** Owl **13)** H. H. Holmes

Across: **8)** Henry Lee Lucas **10)** Jack Unterweger **11)** John Wayne Gacy **14)** Albert Fish **15)** East Area Rapist

NOTORIOUS KILLERS CROSSWORD #2

Across: **5)** Taxidermy **8)** Germany **9)** Tattoos **10)** Cooling off period **11)** Hearse **12)** Strangulation **13)** Harold Shipman

Down: **1)** Joe Metheny **2)** Hybristophilia **3)** Kitty Genovese **4)** Audio book narrator **6)** Diane Downs **7)** USA

KILLING GROUNDS MATCHING GAME

1. Tallahassee, Florida, U.S.A. **2.** British Columbia, Canada **3.** London, England **4.** Milwaukee, Wisconsin, U.S.A. **5.** Rostov Oblast, Russia **6.** Mexico City, Mexico **7.** Düsseldorf, Germany **8.** Perth, Australia **9.** Austria **10.** Henan, China **11.** Colombia **12.** France **13.** Hungary **14.** India **15.** Lombardy, Italy **16.** Kazakhstan **17.** Limburg, Netherlands **18.** Pakistan **19.** Poland **20.** Vietnam

KILLERS' JOBS UNSCRAMBLE

1) Ice cream truck driver
2) Police officer
3) Security system installer
4) Nightclub owners
5) Hot dog vendor
6) Firefighter
7) Birthday clown
8) Journalist
9) Pornography actor
10) Russian language teacher
11) KFC franchise owner
12) Gravedigger
13) Suicide prevention hotline
14) Landscaper
15) Mall Santa
16) Music promoter
17) Pig farmer
18) Professional wrestler
19) Babysitter
20) Chocolate factory worker

KILLERS' NAMES WORD SEARCH

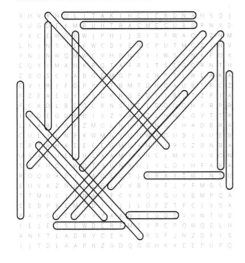

KILLERS' LAST WORDS CRYPTOGRAMS #1–4

1) Peter Kürten

A	B	C	D	E	F	G	H	I	J	K	L	M	N	O	P	Q	R	S	T	U	V	W	X	Y	Z
P	K	Q	M	Y	R	S	J	V	W	A	U	T	O	G	L	F	E	X	Z	D	N	B	I	C	H

"Tell me, after my head has been chopped off, will I still be able to hear, at least for a moment, the sound of my own blood gushing from the stump of my neck? That would be a pleasure to end all pleasures."

2) Aileen Wuornos

A	B	C	D	E	F	G	H	I	J	K	L	M	N	O	P	Q	R	S	T	U	V	W	X	Y	Z
B	I	F	P	Z	G	K	O	E	W	J	Q	N	R	Y	S	A	U	L	C	T	H	V	M	D	X

"I'd just like to say I'm sailing with the rock, and I'll be back like Independence Day, with Jesus, June 6th, like the movie, big mother ship and all. I'll be back."

3) Jake Bird

A	B	C	D	E	F	G	H	I	J	K	L	M	N	O	P	Q	R	S	T	U	V	W	X	Y	Z
F	C	W	A	I	R	J	E	B	L	S	X	U	V	P	N	H	G	T	Y	O	Q	D	M	Z	K

"I'm putting the Jake Bird hex on all of you who had anything to do with me being punished. Mark my words, you will die before I do."

4) James French and George Appel

A	B	C	D	E	F	G	H	I	J	K	L	M	N	O	P	Q	R	S	T	U	V	W	X	Y	Z
W	J	Y	K	T	I	D	E	R	P	G	V	F	X	M	A	C	U	H	S	B	O	Q	Z	L	N

"Hey Fellas! How about this for a headline for tomorrow's paper? French Fries."

"Well Gentlemen, you are about to witness a 'Baked Appel'"

KILLERS' LAST MEALS MATCHING GAME

1) Danny Rolling: Shrimp, lobster, a baked potato, strawberry cheesecake, and sweet tea
2) John Wayne Gacy: A dozen deep-fried shrimp, a bucket of KFC original recipe chicken, fries, and a pound of strawberries
3) Timothy McVeigh: Two pints of mint chocolate chip ice cream
4) Aileen Wuornos: Black coffee
5) Ted Bundy: Nothing
6) Fritz Haarmann: A cigar and a cup of Brazilian coffee
7) Peter Kürten: Wiener schnitzel, fried potatoes, and a bottle of white wine
8) H.H. Holmes: Boiled eggs, toast, and coffee
9) William Bonin: Two pepperoni and sausage pizzas, chocolate ice cream, and three six-packs of Coca-Cola and Pepsi
10) Charles Starkweather: Cold cuts

HISTORICAL CRIMES UNSCRAMBLE

1) Typhoid Mary
2) The Bloody Benders
3) The Kelly Family
4) Servant Girl Annihilator
5) Mary Ann Cotton
6) Burke and Hare
7) Jean Grenier
8) John "liver-eating" Johnson
9) Jane Toppan
10) Belle Gunness
11) Jack the Ripper
12) Hinterkaifek Axe Murders
13) Axeman of New Orleans
14) Delphine LaLaurie
15) Elizabeth Báthory

HISTORICAL CRIMES WORD SEARCH

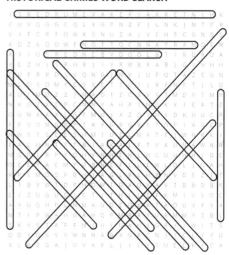

QUIZ – WHAT HAVE YOU LEARNED?

1) Nothing
2) Werewolf
3) Grave robbing
4) Ice cream truck driver
5) Peter Kürten
6) Baked apple
7) Aileen Wuornos
8) Jazz
9) Bloody Benders
10) James French

ALL ABOUT ALIASES

KILLER TO ALIAS MATCHING GAME

1-A, **2**-L, **3**-F, **4**-P, **5**-J, **6**-C, **7**-D, **8**-O, **9**-N, **10**-Q, **11**-S, **12**-E, **13**-T, **14**-I, **15**-G, **16**-H, **17**-M, **18**-B, **19**-R, **20**-K

MURDER MONIKERS CROSSWORD #1

Across: **8)** Green River Killer **9)** KFC **10)** Bible John **11)** Bind, Torture, Kill **12)** Morphine Overdose

Down: **1)** Death by Torture **2)** Butcher Baker **3)** Son of Hope **4)** Floppy Disk **5)** Unabomber **6)** Arthur Leigh Allen **7)** Sixteen

MURDER MONIKERS CROSSWORD #2

Across: **5)** Original Night Stalker **6)** Cecil **7)** France **8)** Geordie

Down: **1)** Boston Strangler **2)** ABC Murders **3)** Demonic Dog **4)** Angel Makers

VICTIM COUNT RANKING GAME

1) E, I, J, C, G, A, B, D, H, F   **2)** B, E, C, D, A, I, F, H, J, G **3)** A, J, D, I, H, E, G, C, F, B

CREEPY QUOTES CRYPTOGRAMS #1–3

John Wayne Gacy

A	B	C	D	E	F	G	H	I	J	K	L	M	N	O	P	Q	R	S	T	U	V	W	X	Y	Z
F	T	A	O	R	J	W	I	Q	U	L	Y	N	M	D	E	S	X	B	P	H	K	Z	V	C	G

"The only thing they can get me for is running a funeral parlour without a license."

Ed Kemper

A	B	C	D	E	F	G	H	I	J	K	L	M	N	O	P	Q	R	S	T	U	V	W	X	Y	Z
J	W	H	I	S	L	D	T	O	X	F	U	Y	P	K	Q	A	V	C	G	N	R	Z	B	M	E

"One side of me says, 'I'd like to talk to her, date her.' The other side of me says, 'I wonder what her head would look like on a stick.'"

John George Haigh

A	B	C	D	E	F	G	H	I	J	K	L	M	N	O	P	Q	R	S	T	U	V	W	X	Y	Z
F	X	K	R	H	N	Y	P	L	G	Q	C	V	T	A	W	J	E	M	O	Z	U	S	B	D	I

"In my dream I see before me a forest of crucifixes which gradually turn into trees. At first there appears to be dew or rain dripping from the branches, but as I approach, I realize it is blood. Suddenly the whole forest begins to writhe. The trees, stark and erect, ooze blood. A man goes to each tree, catching the blood in a cup. When his cup is full, he approaches me: 'Drink' he says, but I am unable to move. '

GRUESOME WORDS WORD SEARCH

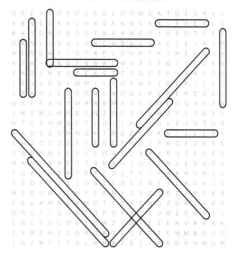

ALSO KNOWN AS WORD SEARCH

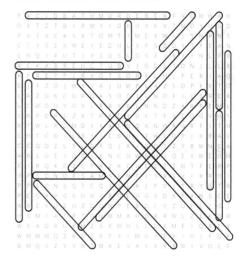

WORLD MAP MATCHING GAME

1. San Francisco, California, U.S.A. **2.** South Africa **3.** London, England **4.** Ontario, Canada **5.** Italy **6.** Glasgow, Scotland **7.** Hungary **8.** Kansas, U.S.A. **9.** Russia **10.** Alaska, U.S.A **11.** Washington State, U.S.A. **12.** Mexico **13.** Brazil **14.** Manchester, England **15.** Australia **16.** China **17.** India **18.** Japan **19.** Kazakhstan **20.** France

YOU CAN CALL ME ... PICTURE PUZZLES

1) Bible John
2) The Original Night Stalker
3) The Vampire of Sacramento
4) The Milwaukee Cannibal
5) Son of Sam
6) The Dating Game Killer

ALIASES UNSCRAMBLE

1) Original Night Stalker
2) Giggling Granny
3) Chessboard Killer
4) Rostov Ripper
5) Son of Sam

6) Bind Torture Kill
7) Doctor Death
8) Metal Fang
9) Brooklyn Vampire
10) Milwaukee Cannibal
11) Zodiac Killer
12) Bible John
13) Jack the Ripper
14) Ken and Barbie Killers
15) Little Old Lady Killer
16) Yorkshire Ripper
17) Boston Strangler
18) Happy Face Killer
19) Green River Killer
20) Killer Clown

QUIZ – WHAT HAVE YOU LEARNED?

1) Ken and Barbie

2) Kazakhstan

3) Original Night Stalker

4) Italy

5) John George Haigh

6) Dennis Rader

7) He had the wrong accent

8) Red

9) Running a funeral parlour without a license

10) Hope

KILLER DUOS

PARTNERS IN CRIME MATCHING GAME

1-G, **2**-J, **3**-Q, **4**-H, **5**-I, **6**-P, **7**-O, **8**-M, **9**-F, **10**-R, **11**-S, **12**-K, **13**-C, **14**-L, **15**-E, **16**-B, **17**-N, **18**-A, **19**-D

PAIRS OF PERIL WORD SEARCH

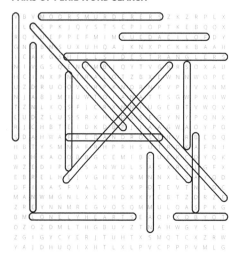

VICTIM COUNT RANKING GAME

G, D, F, I, A, H, B, E, C, J
F, C, E, A, D, B, G, H, I, J

MURDEROUS MULTIPLES CROSSWORD #1

Across: **4)** Baby farming **6)** Quilt **7)** Saddleworth **9)** Candyman **10)** Folie a deux **11)** Ottis Toole **12)** Bonnie and Clyde **13)** Ken and Barbie **14)** Tinder

Down: **1)** Lonely Hearts **2)** Hillside Stranglers **3)** Moorhouse Murders **5)** Fred and Rose West **8)** Judy Garland

MURDEROUS MULTIPLES CROSSWORD #2

Across: **7)** Catherine Lorre **8)** Leopold and Loeb **9)** DC Snipers **12)** Sunset Strip

Down: **1)** Vegetarian Muslim Warriors **2)** Badlands Killers **3)** Seventeen **4)** Rancho El Angel **5)** The Virgin Hunters **6)** Toybox Killer **10)** Columbine High **11)** Sierra Nevada **13)** Sister

CREEPY QUOTES CRYPTOGRAM

Henry Lee Lucas

A	B	C	D	E	F	G	H	I	J	K	L	M	N	O	P	Q	R	S	T	U	V	W	X	Y	Z
X	W	P	N	I	E	F	O	K	G	J	Y	V	S	B	M	D	H	T	R	C	U	A	Q	Z	L

"My victims never knew what was going to happen to them. I've had shooting, knifings, strangulations, beatings, and I've participated in actual crucifixions of humans. All across the country there's people just like me who set out to destroy life."

QUIZ – WHAT HAVE YOU LEARNED?

1) Baby farming
2) Crucifixion
3) Candy Man
4) David and Catherine Birnie
5) Ian Brady and Myra Hindley
6) Paul Bernardo and Karla Homolka
7) Fred and Rose West
8) Chicago
9) Leonard Lake and Charles Ng
10) Peter Lorre

FEMALE KILLERS

FEMME FATALE UNSCRAMBLE

1) Aileen Wuornos
2) Belle Gunness
3) Beverley Allitt
4) Diane Downs
5) Amelia Dyer
6) Myra Hindley
7) Rose West
8) Karla Homolka
9) Delphine LaLaurie
10) Elizabeth Báthory
11) Dorothea Puente
12) Juana Barraza
13) Nannie Doss
14) Lizzie Borden
15) Lavinia Fisher
16) Judy Buenoano
17) Gypsy Rose Blanchard
18) Sara Jane Moore
19) Marguerite Marie Alibert
20) Jane Toppan

FEMALE KILLERS WORD SEARCH

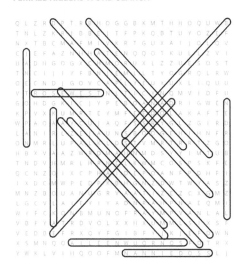

VICTIM COUNT RANKING GAME

1) D, J, H, B, F, G, C, E, A, I
2) D, H, J, G, F, C, E, A, B, I
3) B, I, E, A, C, G, J, D, F/H

LETHAL LADIES CROSSWORD #1

Across: 2) Lavinia Fisher 5) Gerald Ford
6) Mary Ann Cotton 7) Independence Day 10) Rose
West 13) Delphine LaLaurie 14) Blood Countess

Down: 1) Soap bar 3) Wrestler 4) Homolka
8) Personals 9) Money 11) Eleven 12) Manson

LETHAL LADIES CROSSWORD #2

Across: 3) Australia 8) Joanna Dennehy 9) Poison
10) Mother's Friend

Down: 1) Las Poquianchis 2) Judy Buenoano 4) Myra
Hindley 5) Dorothea Puente 6) Pickaxe 7) Flypaper

CREEPY QUOTES CRYPTOGRAM

Jane Toppan and Aileen Wuornos

A	B	C	D	E	F	G	H	I	J	K	L	M	N	O	P	Q	R	S	T	U	V	W	X	Y	Z
P	I	J	B	F	E	U	T	A	Z	S	D	O	C	M	L	V	Y	X	H	R	Q	N	K	W	G

"That is my ambition: to have killed more people
than any man or woman who has ever lived."

"To me, this world is nothing but evil, and my own evil
just happened to come out 'cause of the circumstances
of what I was doing."

QUIZ – WHAT HAVE YOU LEARNED?

1) Delphine LaLaurie and Belle Gunness
2) Lavinia Fisher
3) Flypaper
4) Financial gain
5) To kill more people than any man or woman who
has ever lived
6) 11
7) Poison
8) Elizabeth Báthory
9) Sarah Jane Moore
10) Boarding house

CELEBRITY AND POP CULTURE

ASSASSINS MATCHING GAME

1-D, **2**-L, **3**-J, **4**-H, **5**-B, **6**-R, **7**-A, **8**-Q, **9**-K, **10**-F, **11**-C, **12**-M, **13**-S, **14**-N, **15**-G, **16**-E, **17**-T, **18**-O, **19**-I, **20**-P

FAMED FATALITIES CROSSWORD #1

Across: **6)** Phil Hartman **10)** Don King **11)** Symbionese Liberation Army **12)** Sharon Tate **13)** Burlesque

Down: **1)** Spider **2)** Serial **3)** Sam Cooke **4)** Alias Grace **5)** Phil Spector **7)** Tight End **8)** Nancy Spungen **9)** OJ Simpson

FAMED FATALITIES CROSSWORD #2

Across: **3)** Gianni Versace **5)** The Exorcist **7)** Natalie Wood **9)** Marie Manning **10)** Dominique Dunne **11)** The Staircase **12)** William S. Burroughs

Down: **1)** The Confession Killer **2)** The Dating Game **4)** Las Vegas **6)** Chris Benoit 8) L.A.

MURDER BOOKS MATCHING GAME

1-C, **2**-B, **3**-H, **4**-E, **5**-I, **6**-D, **7**-A, **8**-G, **9**-J, **10**-F

CRIME AND JUSTICE QUOTES CRYPTOGRAMS #1–2

OJ Simpson and Johnnie Cochran

A	B	C	D	E	F	G	H	I	J	K	L	M	N	O	P	Q	R	S	T	U	V	W	X	Y	Z
E	A	S	H	F	P	O	G	W	Z	M	R	U	I	K	V	B	J	T	N	D	L	Y	Q	X	C

"In America you get as much justice as you can afford."

"If it doesn't fit, you must acquit."

Marcia Clark

A	B	C	D	E	F	G	H	I	J	K	L	M	N	O	P	Q	R	S	T	U	V	W	X	Y	Z
L	U	N	S	F	B	Y	T	Z	E	G	Q	K	P	X	R	C	M	W	D	J	A	I	H	O	V

"When the trial began, all of the networks were getting these hate-hail letters because people's soap operas were being interrupted for the Simpson trial, but then . . . people who liked soap operas got addicted to the Simpson trial and they got really upset when the Simpson trial was over."

CELEBRITIES UNSCRAMBLE

1) OJ Simpson
2) Aaron Hernandez
3) Phil Spector
4) Sid Vicious
5) Johnny Lewis
6) Suge Knight
7) Dog the Bounty Hunter
8) Michael Jace
9) Rodney Alcala
10) Don King
11) Chris Benoit
12) Claudine Longet
13) William S. Burroughs
14) Snoop Dogg
15) Robert Blake

NOTORIOUS CASES WORD SEARCH

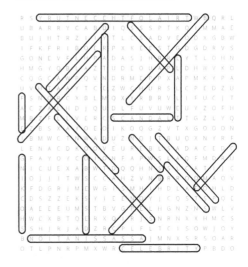

MURDER MOVIES/DOCUSERIES MATCHING GAME

1-M, 2-I, 3-F, 4-N, 5-J, 6-C, 7-B, 8-T, 9-Q, 10-E, 11-S,
12-D, 13-P, 14-G, 15-K, 16-A, 17-R, 18-O, 19-H, 20-L

CRIME SONGS MATCHING GAME

1-J, 2-L, 3-N, 4-A, 5-S, 6-I, 7-Q, 8-B, 9-F, 10-R, 11-M,
12-K, 13-H, 14-G, 15-T, 16-O, 17-C, 18-P, 19-D, 20-E

QUIZ – WHAT HAVE YOU LEARNED?

1) Brenda Ann Spencer
2) Their soap operas were being interrupted
3) Jeffrey Dahmer
4) Danny Rolling
5) *The Exorcist*
6) Lee Harvey Oswald
7) His wife, Brynn Amdahl
8) Gianni Versace
9) "If it doesn't fit, you must acquit"
10) Marie Manning

PARANORMAL TWIST

WICKED WORDS CRYPTOGRAM

Sarah Good

A	B	C	D	E	F	G	H	I	J	K	L	M	N	O	P	Q	R	S	T	U	V	W	X	Y	Z
Q	C	Z	N	T	K	P	A	Y	O	F	U	I	B	J	E	M	L	H	W	R	S	X	V	D	G

"You are a liar. I am no more a witch than you are a wizard, and if you take away my life, God will give you blood to drink."

MYSTERIOUS HAPPENINGS CROSSWORD #1

Across: **4)** Vampire **5)** David Berkowitz **6)** Teresita Basa **7)** Satanic Panic **8)** Hell **9)** Jodie **10)** Pentagram

Down: **1)** Salem **2)** Slenderman **3)** Hammersmith Ghost

MYSTERIOUS HAPPENINGS CROSSWORD #2

Across: **5)** The Devil Made Me Do It **7)** The Exorcism of Emily Rose **9)** Annie Palmer **10)** Eastern State

Down: **1)** Red Barn Murder **2)** Winchester Mystery House **3)** Greenbrier Ghost **4)** Bobby Mackey's **6)** Lemp Mansion **8)** Road House

WEIRD THINGS WORD SEARCH

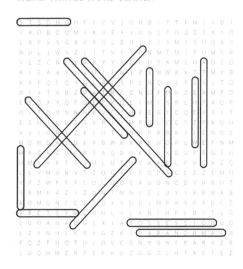

QUIZ – WHAT HAVE YOU LEARNED?

1) Satanic
2) Greenbrier Ghost
3) Alcatraz
4) They tried to use demonic possession as a legitimate defence in court
5) Salem Witch Trials
6) Teresita Basa
7) Red Barn
8) Creepypasta
9) Blood
10) Winchester

CULTS

FATAL FOLLOWERS UNSCRAMBLE

1) The Sullivan Institute
2) Heaven's Gate Away Team
3) Rajneeshpuram
4) Cult Awareness Network
5) The Seven Seals
6) E-Meter
7) Colloidal Silver
8) Lifetime rehabilitation
9) Eternal Mountain
10) International Knighthood

FINAL MESSAGE CRYPTOGRAMS #1-2

Heaven's Gate

A	B	C	D	E	F	G	H	I	J	K	L	M	N	O	P	Q	R	S	T	U	V	W	X	Y	Z
T	I	N	M	H	L	O	C	D	K	V	S	A	R	X	Y	J	U	Q	G	E	Z	B	F	P	W

"Hale-Bopp brings closure to Heaven's Gate...Our 22 years of classroom here on planet Earth is finally coming to conclusion - 'Graduation' from the human evolutionary level. We are happily prepared to leave this world and go with Ti's crew."

Jim Jones

A	B	C	D	E	F	G	H	I	J	K	L	M	N	O	P	Q	R	S	T	U	V	W	X	Y	Z
P	K	H	O	Z	T	L	G	U	D	Y	E	W	F	C	B	J	N	R	V	Q	M	X	A	S	I

"Take our life from us. We laid it down. We got tired. We didn't commit suicide. We committed an act of revolutionary suicide, protesting the conditions of an inhumane world."

FOLLOW THE LEADER CROSSWORD #1

Across: **2)** Nike Decades **4)** Sea Org **8)** Jonestown **10)** Waco Siege **11)** NXIVM **12)** Ti and Do

Down: **1)** Vernon Howell **3)** Teens For Christ **5)** Polygamy **6)** Ant Hill Kids **7)** Flavor Aid **9)** Hale-Bopp

FOLLOW THE LEADER CROSSWORD #2

Across: **2)** Roch Thériault **5)** Dianetics **9)** Flirty Fishing **11)** Synanon **12)** Order of the Solar Temple **14)** Helter Skelter **15)** The Family

Down: **1)** Aum Shinrikyo **3)** Thetan **4)** Circle of Friends **6)** Attack therapy **7)** Allison Mack **8)** Blood atonement **10)** Rajneeshees **13)** Love Has Won

CULT TO LEADER/FOUNDER MATCHING GAME

1-O, **2**-B, **3**-M, **4**-J, **5**-R, **6**-P, **7**-G, **8**-Q, **9**-D, **10**-A, **11**-L, **12**-K, **13**-N, **14**-I, **15**-H, **16**-E, **17**-T, **18**-S, **19**-C, **20**-F

PART OF THE CULT WORD SEARCH

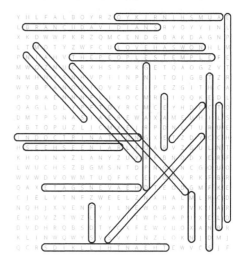

QUIZ – WHAT HAVE YOU LEARNED?

1) Branch Davidians **2)** Mother God **3)** Synanon **4)** Nike Decades **5)** Hale-Bopp **6)** Revolutionary suicide **7)** "Protesting the conditions of an inhumane world" **8)** Ti and Do **9)** Indoctrinating new members into the Children of God through sexual means **10)** NXIVM

THE GOOD GUYS

DOING IT RIGHT CROSSWORD #1

Across: **4)** Amanda Knox **5)** Psychological Profiling
6) West Memphis Three **8)** Ann Rule **9)** Malcolm X

Down: **1)** Central Park Five **2)** Michelle McNamara
3) Innocence Project **7)** Steven Avery

DOING IT RIGHT CROSSWORD #2

Across: **5)** San Antonio Four **8)** Kevin Strickland
9) Reid Technique

Down: **1)** Rubin Carter **2)** Eyewitness testimony
3) Satanic Panic **4)** Forty six years **6)** Steven Truscott
7) Illinois

JUSTICE OR? CRYPTOGRAMS #1-2

MLK and Angela Davis

A	B	C	D	E	F	G	H	I	J	K	L	M	N	O	P	Q	R	S	T	U	V	W	X	Y	Z
N	U	S	K	M	Q	L	A	O	W	R	V	T	I	Y	H	F	E	C	P	B	X	J	Z	D	G

"Injustice anywhere is a threat to justice everywhere."

"Jails and prisons are designed to break human
beings; to convert the population into specimens in
a zoo – obedient to our keepers, but dangerous to
each other."

Bryan Stevenson

A	B	C	D	E	F	G	H	I	J	K	L	M	N	O	P	Q	R	S	T	U	V	W	X	Y	Z
F	O	Z	P	L	S	C	J	K	X	H	Q	T	B	G	W	A	V	R	N	Y	M	I	U	D	E

"Our criminal justice system treats you better if
you are rich and guilty than if you are poor and
innocent."

WRONGFUL CONVICTION RANKING GAME

G, I, E, B, J, A, H, C, D, F
B, D, E, A/C, F, J, G, H, I

INNOCENCE UNSCRAMBLE

1) Miscarriage of Justice
2) Eyewitness Testimony
3) False Confession
4) Forensic Analysis
5) Expert Witness
6) Perjury
7) Confirmation bias
8) Noble Cause Corruption
9) Plea Bargain
10) Innocent Prisoner's Dilemma

FALSE ACCUSATIONS WORD SEARCH

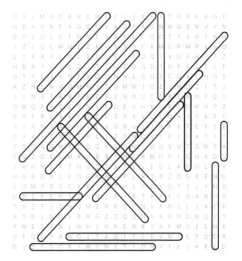

QUIZ - WHAT HAVE YOU LEARNED?

1) Eyewitness testimony
2) Ted Bundy
3) Zoos
4) Marsha Clark
5) Robert Ressler
6) Wrongful imprisonment
7) 44%
8) Noble Cause
9) 46
10) Central Park

ORGANIZED CRIME

MAFIA UNSCRAMBLE

1) The Five Families
2) St. Valentine's Day Massacre
3) Protection Racketeering
4) The Dapper Don
5) Castellammarese War
6) Capo Famiglia
7) Yubitsume
8) The Grim Reaper
9) Witness Protection Program
10) The Corporation

CRIME FAMILIES CROSSWORD #1

Across: **4)** Lucky **6)** Vincent Gigante **8)** Soldier
10) Mussolini **11)** Fats Waller

Down: **1)** Rudy Giuliani **2)** Made Man **3)** Al Capone
5) RICO **7)** Tattoos **9)** Bugsy

CRIME FAMILIES CROSSWORD #2

Across: **4)** Yakuza **5)** New Orleans **6)** The Chin
8) Godfather **9)** Sicily **10)** Geraldo Rivera
11) The Commission **12)** The Dapper Don

Down: **1)** Frank Sinatra **2)** Whitey **3)** Frank Costello
7) Tax evasion

GANGSTERS WORD SEARCH #1

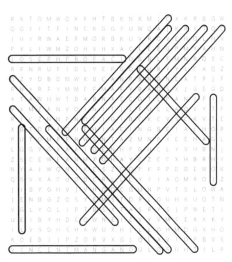

GANGSTERS WORD SEARCH #2

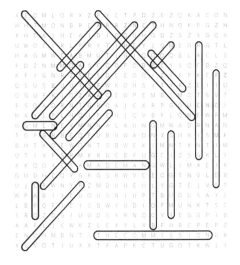

MOBSTER MINDSET CRYPTOGRAMS #1–2

Carlo Gambino and Al Capone

A	B	C	D	E	F	G	H	I	J	K	L	M	N	O	P	Q	R	S	T	U	V	W	X	Y	Z
S	Q	H	B	R	I	A	N	F	O	E	K	U	W	J	Y	M	G	C	P	Z	D	T	L	V	X

"Judges, lawyers and politicians have a license to steal. We don't need one."

"Capitalism is the legitimate racket of the ruling class."

Lucky Luciano and Al Capone

A	B	C	D	E	F	G	H	I	J	K	L	M	N	O	P	Q	R	S	T	U	V	W	X	Y	Z
G	E	I	C	L	S	X	O	Z	U	N	V	R	D	P	Q	K	F	T	M	H	B	Y	W	A	J

"If you have a lot of what people want and can't get, then you can supply the demand, and shovel in the dough."

"You can get much further with a kind word and a gun than you can with a kind word alone."

QUIZ – WHAT HAVE YOU LEARNED?

1) Vincent Gigante
2) Charles Luciano
3) A gun
4) Judges, lawyers, and politicians
5) Yakuza
6) 1970
7) Don Vito Corleone
8) Five
9) Associates
10) Capitalism

UNSOLVED MYSTERIES

MYSTIFYING CASES CROSSWORD #1

Across: **6)** Zodiac Killer **8)** Miyazawa

Down: **1)** Jack the Ripper **2)** Tylenol **3)** JonBenet Ramsey **4)** Panama **5)** Black Dahlia **7)** Tamam Shud **9)** Axe

MYSTIFYING CASES CROSSWORD #2

Across: **2)** Circleville **4)** Beaumont **7)** Mary Celeste **8)** Sodder **9)** Mr. Cruel **10)** Dyatlov Pass **11)** Delphi Murders

Down: **1)** I Can't Believe It's Yogurt! **3)** Elisa Lam **5)** D. B. Cooper **6)** Texarkana

CASE NOT CLOSED UNSCRAMBLE

1) Who Put Bella in the Wych Elm
2) Down the Hill
3) The Town that Dreaded Sundown
4) Is Finished
5) Small Foreign Faction
6) Eight Day Bride
7) Croatoan
8) Malaysia Airlines
9) Everything is Meaningless
10) Spontaneous Human Combustion

STILL SEARCHING WORD SEARCH

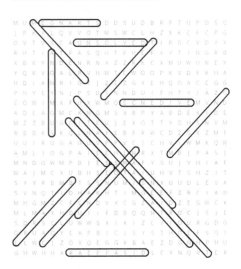

MESSAGES TO VICTIMS CRYPOGRAMS #1–5

Zodiac Cipher

A	B	C	D	E	F	G	H	I	J	K	L	M	N	O	P	Q	R	S	T	U	V	W	X	Y	Z
R	Q	E	M	A	K	Y	J	J	U	H	N	T	O	P	S	F	L	W	Z	I	D	X	V	G	C	B

"I like killing because it is so much fun. It is more fun than killing wild game in the forest because man is the most dangerous animal of all to kill."

D. B. Cooper

A	B	C	D	E	F	G	H	I	J	K	L	M	N	O	P	Q	R	S	T	U	V	W	X	Y	Z
R	V	O	T	G	Z	I	C	D	B	S	M	E	L	Q	K	W	A	H	Y	P	U	X	F	J	N

"I want two hundred thousand dollars by 5PM in cash, exclusively in $20 bills, put in a knapsack. I want two back parachutes and two front parachutes. When we land, I want a fuel truck ready to refuel. No funny stuff or I'll do the job."

Black Dahlia

A	B	C	D	E	F	G	H	I	J	K	L	M	N	O	P	Q	R	S	T	U	V	W	X	Y	Z
C	D	Z	S	V	N	K	T	L	Q	X	R	W	Y	G	F	B	U	E	A	M	H	O	P	I	J

"To whom it may concern. I have waited for the police to capture me for the Black Dahlia killing, but have not. I am too much of a coward to turn myself in, so this is the best way out for me. I couldn't help myself for that, or this. Sorry, Mary"

Circleville Letter

A	B	C	D	E	F	G	H	I	J	K	L	M	N	O	P	Q	R	S	T	U	V	W	X	Y	Z
K	V	U	Y	A	Q	B	R	X	S	H	E	F	G	N	O	C	L	T	P	W	I	J	Z	M	D

"Mrs. Gillispie: Stay away from Massie: Don't lie when questioned about meeting him. I know where you live: I've been observing your house and know you have children. This is no joke. Please take it serious. Everyone concerned has been notified. It will be over soon."

The Watcher

A	B	C	D	E	F	G	H	I	J	K	L	M	N	O	P	Q	R	S	T	U	V	W	X	Y	Z
B	U	V	G	Y	C	Z	X	H	A	P	T	F	O	W	D	N	K	J	E	Q	L	M	S	I	R

"All of the windows and doors in 657 Boulevard allow me to watch you and track you as you move through the house. Who am I? I am The Watcher and have been in control of 657 Boulevard for the better part of two decades now."

QUIZ – WHAT HAVE YOU LEARNED?

1) $200,000
2) Mary
3) The Watcher
4) Texarkana
5) 7
6) Man
7) Wych Elm
8) Delphi Murders
9) Australia Day
10) Christmas

TERRORISM AND MASS INCIDENTS

FEAR AT LARGE CROSSWORD

Across: **2)** State-sponsored **7)** Timothy McVeigh
8) Pennsylvania **10)** Christmas **11)** Amerithrax
12) Reign of Terror

Down: **1)** World Trade Center **3)** Munich **4)** Boston
Marathon **5)** Virginia Tech **6)** Batman **9)** Sarin

TERRORIZED PUBLIC UNSCRAMBLE

1) Radicalization
2) French Revolution
3) Agroterrorism
4) Fearmongering
5) Ideology
6) Biological Warfare
7) Global Terrorism Database
8) Cyberterrorism
9) False Flag Operation
10) Dissident Terrorism

TERRORISM WORD SEARCH

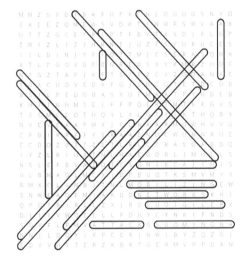

JUSTIFIED TERROR? CRYPTOGRAM

A	B	C	D	E	F	G	H	I	J	K	L	M	N	O	P	Q	R	S	T	U	V	W	X	Y	Z
H	I	V	N	L	B	F	A	G	P	W	S	J	U	Q	X	O	K	R	M	C	D	E	Y	Z	T

"There is the famous statement: 'One man's
terrorist is another man's freedom fighter', but
that is grossly misleading. One can have a perfectly
beautiful cause and yet, if one commits terrorist
acts, it is terrorism regardless."

QUIZ – WHAT HAVE YOU LEARNED?

1) The government
2) Agroterrorism
3) Cyberterrorism
4) State-sponsored
5) The Summer Olympics
6) Freedom fighter
7) Radicalized
8) Tokyo
9) Bioterrorism
10) 1993

CRIMINOLOGY

SCIENCE OF CRIME WORD SEARCH

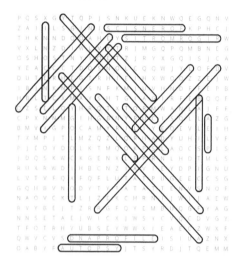

LANGUAGE OF CRIME UNSCRAMBLE

1) Luminol
2) Cesare Lombroso
3) Fingerprints
4) Bench Trial
5) Forensics
6) Blood Spatter
7) Cold Case
8) Accessory
9) Search Warrant
10) Circumstantial Evidence

INVESTIGATION LADDER GAMES #1-4

1) Voir Dire 2) In Cold Blood 3) Serial 4) Israel Keyes
5) OJ Simpson 6) Nilsen 7) Acquittal 8) Rudy Giuliani
9) Yvan Keller

ANSWER: Visionary

1) Mary Celeste 2) Inadmissible 3) Son of Sam
4) Sentence 5) Iceman 6) Ottis Toole 7) New Orleans

ANSWER: Mission

1) Hung jury 2) EARONS 3) Demonology
4) Oklahoma City 5) NXIVM 6) I-95 Killer 7) Subpoena
8) Tax evasion 9) Investigation
10) Cross-examination

ANSWER: Hedonistic

1) Parole 2) Objection 3) Wayne 4) Evidence 5) RICO

ANSWER: Power

QUIZ - WHAT HAVE YOU LEARNED?

1) Modern Criminology
2) 0
3) Search Warrant
4) Circumstantial
5) Luminol
6) An Accessory
7) Forensics
8) Cold Case
9) Mission
10) Hedonistic

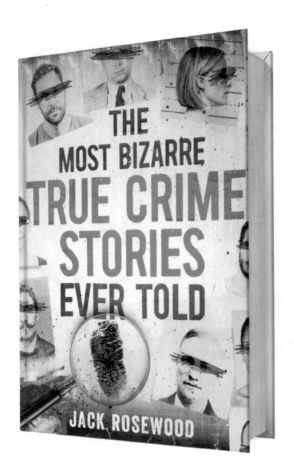

A collection of the most mind-boggling **and** outrageous True Crime cases you've ever read. Stories so bizarre, **creepy** and compelling that you can't stop turning the pages – the **perfect gift** for True Crime lovers.

MORE BOOKS BY JACK ROSEWOOD

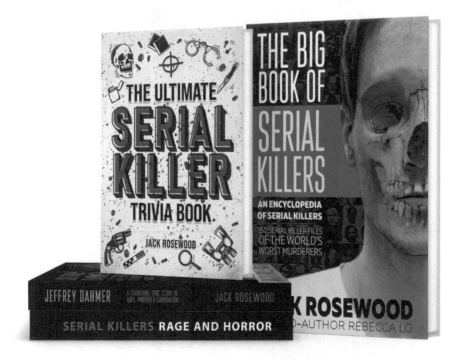

HERE ARE SOME OTHER TITLES YOU MIGHT LIKE:

- Jeffrey Dahmer: A Terrifying True Story of Rape, Murder & Cannibalism

- The Big Book of Serial Killers: 150 Serial Killer Files of the World's Worst Murderers

- Serial Killers Rage and Horror Volume 2:
  8 Shocking True Crime Stories of Serial Killers and Killing Sprees

- The Ultimate Serial Killer Trivia Book: A Collection Of Fascinating Facts And
  Disturbing Details About Infamous Serial Killers And Their Horrific Crimes

BUT WE GOT MANY MORE! GET TWO TRUE CRIME BOOKS FOR FREE!

Check out all of our titles at **www.jackrosewood.com**

Made in United States
Troutdale, OR
11/20/2023

14730269R10086